Arnold Wellmer

Anna, Countess zu Stolberg Wernigerode a story of our own times

Arnold Wellmer

Anna, Countess zu Stolberg Wernigerode a story of our own times

ISBN/EAN: 9783337757137

Hergestellt in Europa, USA, Kanada, Australien, Japan

Cover: Foto ©ninafisch / pixelio.de

Weitere Bücher finden Sie auf **www.hansebooks.com**

ANNA
COUNTESS ZU STOLBERG WERNIGERODE

LADY SUPERINTENDENT OF "BETHANY" DEACONESS HOUSE, AT BERLIN

A Story of Our Own Times

TRANSLATED FROM THE GERMAN OF ARNOLD WELLMER

By D. M. P.

STRAHAN AND CO.
56, LUDGATE HILL, LONDON
1873

LONDON:
PRINTED BY VIRTUE AND CO.
CITY ROAD.

CONTENTS.

CHAP.		PAGE
I.	THE ADMISSION	1
II.	ANNA'S ANCESTRY	11
III.	PETERSWALDAU	29
IV.	KREPPELHOF	43
V.	COLOGNE—DIERSFORDT, KREPPEL—DUSSELDORF—MAGDEBURG	55
VI.	BERLIN	71
VII.	BERLIN—WERNIGERODE—KREPPELHOF	88
VIII.	SISTER ANNA AT BETHANY	96
IX.	MOTHER ANNA IN BETHANY	114
X.	SOUTH GERMANY—ALSACE—SWITZERLAND	126
XI.	ALTONA—FLENSBURG—GORLITZ	132
XII.	RHEIN	161
XIII.	BETHANY	178
XIV.	CONCLUSION	191

CHAPTER I.

THE ADMISSION.

OUT yonder in the Köpnicker fields, to the east of Berlin, surrounded by pleasant gardens and wide lawns, there stands a stately building with high tower, and wide-spreading, airy wings—the hospital and deaconess house of Bethany.

This house of mercy, which is used for nursing the sick, and for training young women to minister efficiently to the sick bodies and souls of their poor brethren, was one of the earliest erections of that large-hearted king, Frederick William IV. of Prussia.

There were deaconesses in the very earliest ages of the Christian Church, who, as handmaidens of the Lord, were responsible for the care of the sick and the poor in the congregations; and we find the title applied by St. Paul to Phœbe, who had proved herself to be indeed a true servant or deaconess of "the church which was at Cenchrea." In the course of centuries, and owing to the decline of Christianity, the office became universally ignored. Suddenly, in the loving heart of a single pastor, in a poor little town on the Rhine, there arose a burning desire to renew it, and God gave this solitary man (uninfluential though he was) power for the work. In 1836, Pastor Fliedner was enabled to open his modest deaconess house at Kaiserswerth—a mere seed of corn, but one planted in God's own fruitful soil!

The Crown Prince of Prussia, Frederick

William, watched with friendly sympathy, first the sowing of this tiny seed, then the striking of its roots, and then the powerful tree which began to spring up. He helped to water it diligently and to shield it from storms; and hardly had he ascended the throne of Prussia and thus acquired kingly power, before it became the heartfelt desire of the young monarch to transplant a sturdy offshoot from the tree on the Rhine to his own capital, and there to tend it and care for it with his own hands.

Endowed with the large means of its royal founder, the deaconess "mother house" of Bethany was able to open its doors to the sick poor and their nurses on October 10th, 1847. No earthly recompense was offered to attract the deaconesses to this home of sickness and heavy labour; yet they came from all sides, rich and poor, high and low, just drawn by their earnest longing to serve their Lord and Saviour in the persons of his poor brethren. Nothing but this motive could have given strength for the devotion and self-denial involved in ceaseless work by the bedsides of strange, rough men; nothing but this earnest longing could have transformed such work into a source of real happiness. And thus began the labours of the Marthas and Marys in the Bethany of the Prussian capital. It was Mary that anointed the Lord with ointment and wiped his feet with her hair, she sat at Jesus' feet and heard his words. Martha was sometimes cumbered with much serving, but Mary and Martha alike devoted themselves most faithfully to the nursing of their sick brother Lazarus at Bethany.

* * * * *

It was the 3rd of June, 1853. In the large garden at Bethany the young shrubs and trees were clad in green, and the elders and other flowering plants were radiant in beauty and sweetness. Some convalescent patients were passing up and down in the pretty grounds, dressed in the blue costume of the institution, or were sitting on the terrace rejoicing in the spring air and sunshine. Just then a perfectly dazzling equipage swept over the Köpnicker fields, which were at that time almost free from houses. A black stag on a gold ground and two red trout on a silver shield decorated the panels. A young lady, whose features were expressive of great character and true sweetness, rose suddenly from the back seat as if impatient of expectation, and looked out of the open window; her large brown eyes sparkled as they gazed lovingly at the tower with the two bells and the bright windows of Bethany, and then turning to the two dear old faces sitting opposite to her in the carriage, she exclaimed, in a voice of deep emotion, while her beautiful eyes filled with tears and she pressed their hands in hers, "Thank you, thank you, darling father and mother, for this hour; may God bless us and the poor sick ones in that house!"

The carriage stops before the stately doors of the institution. The elder lady is assisted to descend by a tall man of about sixty, with a noble figure and mild, refined features; the younger lady has already run up the stone steps. At the sound of the bell the porteress-sister comes out of her room to the left and opens the door. A peaceful smile breaks over her quiet face, surrounded by its white deaconess cap. Sister Regine has long expected and looked forward to this visit.

"Sister Regine, how is the dear Mother to-day?"

"She has had another bad night, one painful night after another, and yet she is never impatient or irritable."

The quiet face in the close cap becomes still quieter. They enter the hall. A large glass cupboard, filled with books, here offers its contents for sale. When the body is cured of sore sickness, and is able to leave this house where it was cured, it is often just the time when the sick soul is most prepared to take a book with it likely to cure it too.

"The mother expects you, I need not announce you," said sister Regine, returning to her work.

The young visitor thanks her cordially, and goes forward a few steps, as if in a well-known place, towards a room opening from the hall. She gently opens the door, and finds herself in the large workroom of the superintendent, which is well decorated with flowers. It is empty. For the last three quarters of a year Bethany's first and dearly-loved "mother," Marianne von Rantzan, has been confined to a couch of bitter pain; and now in a small chamber, beneath the picture of the Holy Saviour, there smiles a delicate white face whose preternaturally large eyes give a loving welcome to the visitor.

Crying softly, the girl bends over the sufferer, and presses a warm kiss on the almost transparent hands.

"We have come to-day, madame, to bring to you our daughter Anna; her God and her heart draw her to this house of mercy, to serve her Saviour in his sick brethren as a faithful handmaiden. We, her parents, pray for the Lord's best blessings on her determination."

"Amen!" bursts from the white lips of the sufferer, as she presses a motherly kiss on the smooth brow of the girl who is kneeling by the side of the bed. "Your Anna will be a .daughter to me!" Then the trembling hands tenderly smooth the rich brown hair from the youthful forehead, and she places on her head a simple white cap, after which they remain a long while folded in each other's arms praying silently for a blessing.

The carriage with the bounding black stag on the gold ground carried back the Count Anton zu Stolberg Wernigerode, Prussian Lieutenant-General, Minister of the Royal Horse, Knight of the high Order of the Black Eagle, and his wife the Countess Louise, to the Minister's hotel in the Wilhelm Strasse.

By the sick bed of Marianne von Rantzan at Bethany there stood, in a scanty black woollen dress, relieved · by a narrow linen collar, her abundant hair almost covered by a close white cap, the youngest probationer in the house. Sister Anna!

No other title did the daughter of Stolberg bear in that house of mercy. She had laid aside all earthly distinctions.

CHAPTER II.

"As for me and my house, we will serve the Lord."
—JOSHUA xxiv. 15.

ON October 15th, 1822, the Countess Augusta Bernstorff Stolberg (sister of the poet-brothers Christian and Frederick Leopold zu Stolberg) wrote to Goethe, who, though she had never seen him, had been her friend from her youth, in touching anxiety about the soul of this noble, cold, worldly-wise, and almost deified "Jupiter Apollo of Weimar," entreating him to forsake the vanities and trifles of this world.

With a spirit of true friendship she says: "Dear, dear Goethe, seek Him who so willingly allows Himself to be found! Believe in Him in whom we" (her dead brothers and herself) "have believed all our lives. The departed ones would add, 'On Him on whom we are gazing now.' And I can tell you, He is the life of my life, the light of my troubled days; He has been the way, the truth, and the life, our Lord and our God, to all three of us."

This faith, firm as a rock, was the foundation on which the ancient race of Stolberg built its house many centuries ago. The origin of the Count's family is lost in the darkness of the Middle Ages, but as early as the eleventh century we find the Thuringian branch of Stolberg flourishing firmly. They proceeded among the first Crusaders from their richly-favoured home to the Holy Land, to purify its territories from the bands of the unbelievers, and to bleed and die in the cause. The Stolbergs encamped before Jerusalem, and were some of the bravest of the Templars or Knights of St. John. They carried with them among the wonders of Palestine the thought of their beautiful fatherland, and while far away still longed for it.

To this day is handed down from mouth to mouth the old story of the knightly Count Stolberg, almost the last of the misguided Crusaders, who, deeply grieved after the loss of Ptolemais, and longing for his fair Thuringian lands, gave utterance to his feelings in a well-known song.

After the death of the Count Henry of Wernigerode, the inhabitants of this rich territory chose as their ruler one of their older reigning line the Count of Stolberg Wernigerode. The two branches of Stolberg-Gedern and Stolberg-Schwarza soon died out, and their possessions fell in to Weringerode. The other branches bloom still in the families of Stolberg-Stolberg and Stolberg-Rossla.

When the "Wittemberg Nightingale" sounded his wonderful notes, the Stolbergs, the descendants of the old Crusaders, were among the first who received the blessed song with open ears and hearts. And when the Reformer came to the Harz Mountains and preached in the little chapel of Falkenstein and in the church of Nordhausea, the Stolbergs sat at his feet, and to this day they follow in the holy ways he taught. Only two departed from them, and they grieved the other Stolbergs to the depth of their hearts. On Whit Sunday, 1800, the poet Frederick Leopold, Count of Stolberg, went over to the Romish Church in the chapel of the Princess Gallitzin in Munster.

Even this Stolberg was a sincerely pious man, full of the warmth of fervent Christian faith and glowing with religious enthusiasm. He used to say, "I and my house will serve the Lord;" and even in the worst times of religious deadness (the days of the French Revolution), he came forward as a faithful and fearless confessor of Christianity. "It grieves and oppresses me when I see the people thinking they can live without God," he wrote to Jacobi. The religious life burned in him more vigorously than even the intimate friendship which had united him since the happy days of his youth with John Henry Voss. But he had a weak, vacillating character and a still weaker heart. He saw in Munster a Romish church in which the predominant features of Popery were almost forgotten. He met there the noblest Catholic men, the Minister of Fürstenberg, the Princess Gallitzin, and the priest Overburg; he grew to love them, and this love made him gild over the deformities of the Papacy, and made him hope to find in the strange Church the rest which his unquiet heart could not find in the Church of his fathers. But did he entirely renounce Lutheranism when he entered the Romish Church? No! his mental conflict continued to the end of his life, and he actually endeavoured to spread far and wide among his people, as a precious book of instruction, Luther's translation of the Bible.

His " History of the Religion of Jesus Christ" worked as usefully in the spread of religious truth among Protestants as among Catholics, and so did the "Meditations on the Holy Scriptures" which he published in his sixty-ninth year. The Bible, a forbidden fruit to the Romish laity, remained the dearest book of this Count Frederick Leopold to the end. "Brought up by godly parents in the study of the Holy Scriptures from childhood, I early loved them and have never ceased to read them," said he in his old age. And from this Bible he, in his seventieth year, sang his dying song with youthful fervour, calling it his "little book of love because it told so much of the Divine love; and when his last hour came, he, the Catholic, strengthened himself for his heavenward journey with the truly evangelical hymn of Paul Gerhardt—"If I should ever leave Thee, yet, Lord, forsake me not." So after all, and notwithstanding his errors, Count Frederick Leopold seems to have been a child of God.

The second Stolberg who forsook Luther's doctrines was the Count Frank, son of Frederick Leopold's daughter. On the other hand, Count Henry Ernest of Helberstadt, who in the middle of the last century sang beautiful religious songs, and wrote "Reflections for Sundays and Festivals," was a most gifted Protestant poet.

Thus there breathed over the race of Stolberg from generation to generation, the blessing of a truly religious atmosphere, and this continues to be the case to the present day. This feeling animated the reigning

Count Christian Frederick of Stolberg Wernigerode as strongly at the beginning of the present century as it had animated his ancestors of Wernigerode in the village among the Harz Mountains. His wife Augusta Eleanora zu Stolberg-Stolberg was a cousin of the poet-brothers Stolberg, and his son Ferdinand married Maria Agnes, the only daughter of Frederick Leopold, who had not gone over to the Romish Church with her parents. Beloved by his people and his ten children, the old Count Christian Frederick lived in his beautiful Harz home, surrounded by the forests and legends and hills of his childhood, a simple happy life. But the aged man was not permitted to sleep beneath the rustle of the Harz forest trees up in the birthplace of his family.

The French Revolution threw its dark shadow over Germany, and the fatherland grew darker and darker. A political and at the same time a religious dispute began to separate the poor Germans more and more hopelessly from each other. Their Church, their Bible, their God became strange to the people, and thus were snapped the holiest bonds which unite member to member in each family, and family to family in each people. The conscience of the German nation seemed to pass away. Its sins cried with ever-increasing loudness to heaven, and there God sat in judgment. They had forgotten Him; He had to show them that He was still there. He stretched out his hand over the poor, foolish, fallen people. The hand held a many-edged sword—Napoleon! This sword fell on the people's neck, heavily, fearfully, till the worn-out sufferers humbled themselves and bowed their necks under the cruel yoke. Then God in his pitying love shattered the terrible sword, and it broke like a blade of grass; and chained the mighty one to the cold rock of St. Helena, out in the wide ocean. But before this, many tears and many warm drops of blood had to flow to the ground. The old Count Christian Frederick of Wernigerode did not murmur against the chastisement of God, but his German heart bled for the sufferings of the people. He did not simply fold his hands in idle sorrow. He himself was too old to draw his sword against the enemy, but he sent his sons to the fight, and his daughters to the hovels of the poor and desolate, and to the beds of the sick and wounded soldiers.

One of the poisonous stabs entered into the very heart of Germany, when the powerful Jerome Napoleon seized the very core of the German provinces, the kingdom of Westphalia. And then the frivolous, insatiable usurper stretched out his hand to the castle of Cassel and bore another pearl from the crown of Prussia. The possessions of Count

Wernigerode formed part of the kingdom of Westphalia. But how could a Stolberg do homage to a Jerome? Could a Stolberg fight under French colours against his German brothers? The Stolbergs broke their swords in pieces and withdrew themselves in deep sorrow to the green solitudes of their Harz Mountains, true to their last breath to their King Frederick William III.

This caused great annoyance at Cassel. The French tyrant in the old castle directed his keen scent over towards the Harz, and he soon discovered what he hoped for, a secret movement among the audacious counts in favour of their lawful sovereign. The youngest son of the elder branch of the family, Anton Stolberg, though only twenty-four years of age, seemed particularly dangerous to him, for he had already fought against the French yoke in the disastrous fields of Saalfeld and Jena, and had bravely distinguished himself in many bloody battles during the succeeding winter's campaign; so the Napoleonic satrap mockingly proclaimed the Count Anton of Stolberg Wernigerode an outlaw, and set a price on his head.

But he had not counted in this matter on the fidelity of the Harz people, which proved stronger than the rocks of their mountains, and purer than the noble metals in the deep mines of their fatherland. Nobody could be found to earn the heavy price of blood, though numbers knew where their Count Anton had hid himself among their hills from the French hangmen.

His native country became increasingly distasteful to the Count Christian Frederick in consequence of the Westphalian usurpation. With some tears in his eyes he left the old birthplace of the counts, his own cradle, and the cradle of his ten children;

but as he turned back to have one last look at the coat of arms over the door, a word flashed before his eyes and sank into his knightly heart, the century-old motto of the Stolbergs, "Spes nescia falli." Hope never maketh ashamed! Hope which is founded on God! And with a blessing on the house of his fathers, with a prayer for the whole oppressed German people and for the mourning royal family, the old Stolberg turned from the house of his fathers for ever! His wife, his children, his children's children, and his faithful servants followed him to the peaceful solitude of the Silesian mountains, where they had other fair possessions. He himself took up his residence in the beautiful old castle of Peterswaldau, near Reichenbach, from the windows of which he could gaze at the picturesque mountains lying before him, and be reminded with a pleasant sadness· of the forsaken Harz mountains. To this house the young Count Anton conducted his bride, Louisa, daughter of the Prussian minister Von der Reck, in 1809, and soon there sprung up around Count Christian Frederick a fresh bright circle of grandchildren, who clung closely to him until his blessed death.

Hope never maketh ashamed! The faithful God did not permit the Stolbergs to be ashamed of their motto! In their quiet retreat they hoped (not in vain) that God would cause the sun of his grace to shine once more over the poor distracted fatherland, and would enable them to exchange the French yoke for a golden day of freedom. Till then, each Stolberg remained bravely waiting, and exhorting his followers to assist in the raising of the Prussian royal house from its present ruin into its ancient glory and strength; and at this patriotic work they laboured courageously in open day, for their frank knightly character revolted from any secret plots or confederations.

Hope never maketh ashamed! and so, before the Stolbergs had hoped, the judgments of God broke over the God-defying. The cruel burning of Moscow was the signal for Germany's uprising. Everywhere a new Spring burst out over the German land. One feeling, one rage, one belief, one confidence began to animate the whole people. The grey-haired poet-brothers Stolberg seized their harps (as their swords were too heavy for them now) and struck them powerfully in the cause of the freedom of their fatherland. Frederick Leopold sent four sons to the Prussian army at the first call of the king, and very soon all the Stolbergs able to fight were found there. Frederick Leopold's son Christian fell at Ligny. "The Lord hath done all things well, He hath rewarded my Christian for his faithful service; so the place is empty where my eyes used to see him, and my heart is sorely wounded, but I have so much cause to praise God that I can still count myself a happy father. He is with our Saviour beside the river of love, for he trusted only in his grace and mercy." This was what the father said when the messenger from victorious Waterloo announced to him the death of his son.

Count Christian Frederick's youngest son, Anton, was wounded at Gros-Gorschen, but while still using crutches he caused himself to be lifted on to his horse, and fought at Lowenberg, Pilgrainsdorf, Goldberg, Katzbach, and Leipsic. He went through the campaign of 1814 and 1815, and the Iron Cross, Class I. and II., adorned his hero breast when, after the peace, he returned as a commander to his aged parents, his youthful bride, and his five blooming children in the castle of Peterswaldau.

After this he devoted himself zealously to works of peace. His grey-haired and almost blind father gave to his sons, Frederick and Anton, possession of the rich territories of Peterswaldau and Kreppelhof— thirteen villages with nearly ten thousand inhabitants. It became the great object of the two brothers to bestow all the blessings of peace on their people. The Stolbergs had always been kind-hearted towards the poor. Count Christian Günther, the father of the poet-brothers, was the first of his rank who granted personal liberty to his servants. Count Anton could not liberate any of his peasants, for his father had already given all their freedom; but there were many other wounds to heal which the war had caused, and many vultures to be stopped from preying on the people, and to these objects he devoted himself heart and soul. He caused churches and schools to be quickly built, applied himself diligently to the improvement of the agricultural and domestic affairs of his province, and assisted and improved, wherever he could. Peterswaldau became a harbour of refuge to all the suffering and oppressed, far and near, and they found in the old castle open hands and open hearts.

And with ever-increasing strength and clearness did the sincere, true Christianity of Count Stolberg develop; with ever-increasing distinctness did he carry the colours of God and his Church; and with ever-increasing joyfulness did his family join in his resolution, "As for me and my house we will serve the Lord."

CHAPTER III.

PETERSWALDAU.

"So is the kingdom of God, as if a man should cast seed into the ground."—MARK iv. 26.

IN the castle at Peterswaldau, on September 6th, 1819, was born to Count Anton and the Countess Louise their eighth child and fifth daughter, our Anna.

We know but little of her childhood. Those who were watching her unfolding before their eyes did not care to talk much about her to others. But to the end of her life she loved to speak of the happy days of her youth, when she was surrounded by such an atmosphere of true living faith that she seemed almost to imbibe it with her daily life.

Childhood is certainly the most fertile soil and season, and is rich in promise of a rewarding harvest. This thought often encouraged her parents and grandparents to plant (like faithful gardeners) seeds of corn from God's kingdom in the spring land of the child's heart, and they were permitted to see what was thus sown in her, take root, and bloom, and ripen, and bear rich golden grain. They daily saw in her the promise fulfilled, "If ye walk in my statutes and keep my commandments and do them, then I will give you rain in due season, and the land shall yield her increase, and the trees of the field shall yield their fruit."

A deep feeling of thankfulness filled her heart to her last hours that she had been able from her earliest years to look up to those she most loved on earth, and she invariably clung to her parents with the most reverent love and the most child-like obedience. Certainly the old Count Christian's was a beautifully patriarchal life at Peterswaldau, at the side of his wife and in the midst of his children and grandchildren, his whole manner so Christ-like, so noble, so perfectly loving.

A warm German feeling animated this house so rich in children. The mother and grandmother moved gently and quietly about their own house and in the huts of the poor, and the children were early allowed to share in this work of blessing. Each little one had a heart for the misery and suffering around it, and noble grains of seed were dropped into its tender soil. It was considered a special reward and distinction to be permitted to accompany the mother on a quiet errand of mercy and love, carrying a little basket containing food for the hungry, or delicacies for the sick, or clothing for the naked. And thus the first seeds of active brotherly love were planted in each little heart, and God gave the early and the latter rain and the warm sunshine, and so the little seed fructified. The father helped diligently in the work of watering and tending. His noble, mild, courteous bearing, his sincere piety, his daily acts of self-denial, his unwearying readiness to help others, formed a bright example for his children.

Their manner of bringing up could hardly have been simpler in a burgher house. Dressed in linen frocks spun in a loom in the village, and without any ornament, the Count's children played merrily and harmlessly under the fine old trees of the park, while, with her work in her hand, their mother sat by guiding and watching over them.

In later years the Countess Anna used to recall with feelings of some regret the light, cool summer dress of her childhood; she lamented the change that had taken place meanwhile, and the punctilious care for the poor covering of the dying body! A drive with their parents in the country, an expedition to the neighbouring mountains or into the forest, were the children's greatest treats on their birthdays; a bunch of grapes from the hands of their parents or grandparents their most costly present.

It was a very joyful event in their child world when the mother of their governess, Cleophea Schlatter, sent two books for her daughter's pupils from her far distant shop behind the tower at St. Gall; they were the "Basket of Flowers," and "Rosa of Jannenberg," by the author of "Easter Eggs."

Money-boxes were only possessed by the children to be quickly emptied by them into the hands of the poor.

The simplest and most wholesome food for

soul and body was their daily nourishment, and so they grew up with sound, healthy bodies and minds.

Yet in this house there were not wanting those pure fragrant flowers which so beautify life. The aged Countess Augusta Eleanora was a woman as intellectual as she was spiritual. She was in constant correspondence with Lavater and John M. Sailer, and she bequeathed this friendship to her son Anton, who exchanged many letters with the latter.

The poet-brothers Stolberg carefully nursed in their family the flower of poetry. As Dean of the Cathedral at Halberstadt, Count Christian Frederick was obliged to spend some winter months in the town. The author of "Grenadier Lieder" was a very welcome visitor at the Deanery, and he used to bring with him whichever of his many poet friends he had managed to stow away in his tiny house, which like a little nest was never empty of German poets needing help.

Frequently, too, the brothers Christian and Frederick Leopold revisited the village of the Stolberg Wernigerodes; these were true feast-days of poetry. Music was also diligently practised among the numerous children at the Harzburg. The young Count Anton played several instruments in the family concerts, and was particularly fond of the soft yet full notes of the violoncello. When as a cornet he arrived in Dresden in 1801, to be prepared for his entrance into the Prussian Body Guard, he was an almost daily visitor at the hospitable house of the Körners, where art and science flourished greatly, and where Frederick Schiller spent so many happy days.

Such were among the fair flowers that beautified the quiet, peaceful childhood of the young Countess Anna; she was refreshed by their loveliness and fragrance, and she grew up like a very sweet blossom herself.

Count Anton and the Countess chose their children's teachers with the most anxious solicitude, for they knew that the more fertile is the soil the more abundant will be its noxious weeds if the gardener be unfaithful.

In the spring of 1820 there arrived in Germany from St. Gall a young lady full of life and earnestness. This was Cleophea Schlatter, a daughter of, the pious Anna Schlatter, "in the shop behind the tower of St. Gall," who, notwithstanding a poor education, was in correspondence with such men as Bishop Sailer, Lavater, Boos, and Gossner, and whose letters flew through Germany to the refreshment of many weary hearts. The Crown Prince of Prussia, Frederick William, read a copy of one of these simple, powerful letters, and ordered its publication. Count Anton begged for permission to circulate copies of her letters to the cantons of Waldhaüser and Haszlingen on the persecution of the witness Boos, feeling they would benefit weak believers. The Duchess of Wurtemberg often visited her dear friend "in the little shop behind the tower." This mother gave her daughter Cleophea an open letter when she set off on her journey through Germany. It was as follows :—

"If my dear daughter, Cleophea Schlatter, on her way from St. Gall to Germany, has the happiness of meeting with unexpected friends, who for the sake of Christ our Lord would wish to show her a kindness, I greet them through her with heartfelt love, and pray them to give my child a word or a look of blessing, and to receive her as myself. Our Lord and Master will, in his great love, regard as done to Himself what is done to the least of his disciples. Grace and peace from God the Father and Christ our Lord be with all who love Him.

"ANNA SCHLATTER.

"March 14, 1820."

With this letter of recommendation, Cleophea Schlatter soon entered the castle of Peterswaldau as governess to the young Countess. She is described as being "very artless and unacquainted with the ways of the fashionable world, a simple maiden without rank or honour or wealth, but one who had Christ as her King;" and because of this common allegiance the governess was treated in the Count's house as a daughter and sister. "The dear gentle Countess silently pressed my hand," wrote Cleophea, with reference to a religious conversation, "and we became bound together for eternity!" The joyful natural child of the Swiss mountains entered like a fresh spring of happiness into the beautiful child-life at Peterswaldau, and scattered refreshing, nourishing drops of blessing on all sides, and especially on the human blossoms entrusted to her. From her distant home, Anna Schlatter earnestly exhorted her daughter to beware of the little frivolities of the world. She thus writes to Cleophea: "I advise you as strongly as I can to impress upon the young ladies entrusted to you, that it is a proof of great mental weakness to lay any greater value upon dress than as it serves for purposes of warmth and covering; our great object, during our short lifetime should be the acquirement of a far higher kind of ornament, the ornament of a meek and quiet spirit."

She thus addressed the tutor of the young Count, the Candidate Adolf Zahn, in watchful love for the young children whom she had never herself seen: "Dear brother Zahn! May our Lord Jesus bless your training of the tender plants, watering them and causing the house of Stolberg to grow into a tree of righteousness, whose shadow and fruitfulness will bring glory to God throughout a wide circle!"

Four years afterwards the children had to be separated from their teachers. Adolf Zahn was called to be the pastor of a church by the Baron Kottwitz, a friend of Neander's. There on the Pomeranian coast a wonderful spiritual movement arose. Cleophea soon went thither too as Zahn's bride. Her grateful and affectionate pupils were very anxious to console themselves, at least in a measure, by twining the bridal wreath in their beloved Cleophea's hair at Peterswaldau; but the congregation in Pomerania longed so ardently for their young pastor, that Adolf Zahn had to hurry from his examination at Berlin to his wedding. Cleophea accompanied him at once, and before many years their labours were crowned with much blessing.

Very soon another young Swiss came to the Stolbergs' house in Cleophea's place; one highly gifted in intellect, and still more gifted in heart—Mademoiselle Guyenet. Her influence fell especially on Anna, with whom she remained for seven years as a teacher and friend. A faithful correspondence, continued to the end of her life, cemented the bond still more firmly, and to her grave Anna Stolberg remained united to the guide of her youth by the warmest love and gratitude.

"The love of God is the best wisdom!" This was the rule by which Count Anton chose his children's preceptors, and so they earnestly helped the parents in sowing the seed in the young hearts; and the old word of Luther was exemplified by every one in the house, old and young—" If each one leavens his part, the lump will prove good."

CHAPTER IV.

KREPPELHOF.

" There is a friend that sticketh closer than a brother."
—PROV. xviii. 24.

IN the spring of 1824 the grandfather, Count Christian Frederick, went home to his fathers. His end was as bright and peaceful as his life had been; and six years previously he had had the joy of celebrating his "golden wedding" in the midst of his children and grandchildren. His eldest son, Henry, succeeded to the title. Count Frederick inherited Peterswaldau and eight villages; Count Constantin, Jannowitz and six villages; and the youngest son, Anton, the estate of Kreppelhof, at the foot of the Riesengebirge.

The next year he and his family migrated to the castle there. His ceaseless activity as a landlord proved a great blessing to his whole territory, and, indeed, far beyond it. The purity of his heart and character, the noble firmness and manly trustworthiness of his conduct and actions, combined with his great personal attractiveness and honest benevolence, caused high and low, rich and poor, to rally round their new lord with the greatest confidence. His wife and daughters found a large sphere of usefulness in the five villages belonging to Kreppelhof and in the huts of the poor weavers of the Riesengebirge.

At this period the parents, for the sake of the children, cultivated the acquaintance of several neighbouring noble families. These friendships were, however, no new thing; they had been formed and maintained during the time of Germany's oppression under Napoleon's tyranny, and had been continued in the happy season of Germany's deliverance; so the children had the heroes and heroines of other times before their eyes as an example.

In the cool mountain air of the castle of Fischbach, the Prince and Princess William of Prussia (bright double stars in Prussia's most troubled skies) sought a summer refreshment from the golden prison of Berlin life, and frequently lingered there with their children till Christmas.

The friendship between the Prince and Count Anton was already an old one, as it had arisen from a little incident in their young happy days as soldiers. The Count was a lieutenant in the Garde du Corps at Berlin in 1803, when Prince William entered the regiment. The gay and youthful royal blood did not trouble itself particularly about the dry commissariat and stabling department of the army, but the stern, grave soldier, King Frederick William III., required all the details of the routine business from every prince of his house.

One day he visited the riding school of the Garde du Corps and examined his young brother in the names of the horses. Prince William was in the direst confusion; he only knew the name of his own horse, and that the King did not ask him. Suddenly he saw a sub-lieutenant drawing letters in the sand of the riding-school with the stick which all officers carried at that time; he spelt them with a hasty glance, and was able to tell the King the name of every horse.

Prince William never forgot this friendly act of Anton Stolberg's. When called to war he selected him as his adjutant, and side by side the Prince and the Count fought at almost all the battles and victories in the war of freedom. In the battle of Lützen, where Prince William threw himself at a critical moment at the head of the Prussian army, the horses of himself and his adjutant were killed under them. Count Anton fell to the ground with his horse; smothered by the weight of the beast, trampled on by the hoofs of the cavalry, he remained bleeding and insensible on the field, and like those other heroes of German liberty, Scharnhorst and Prince Leopold of Hesse Homberg, must have sealed this victory with his blood, if the Prince had not searched for his friend among the dead and caused him to be removed and cared for. Count Anton insisted, notwithstanding his bandages, in being lifted (however painfully) on to his horse again, and the young soldiers fought once more side by side, and in the storming of the village of Athis secured the victory of Laon. After the unhappy battles of Jena and Austerlitz, Prince and Princess William offered themselves to the tyrant in Paris as hostages for the enormous tribute which the victors had laid on the exhausted Prussians, and Count Anton wished to accompany his friends thither. Napoleon did not accept the hostages; he wished for gold—bloody gold!

In the year 1810, when the swords were resting in inactivity, Prince William and Count Anton travelled together to Silesia, to inform themselves with their own eyes and ears about the state of the people.

They fought together again in the campaigns of 1813 and 1814, and took part in the triumphal entrance into Paris; and when the prisoner of Elbe, with a gamester's despair, staked his last chances on a final throw, Prince William himself fetched his faithful adjutant from the village of Stolberg Wernigerode to the new victory at Belle Alliance.

This friendship of war was renewed in peace

Anna, Countess of Stolberg. 49

when, in 1822, Count Anton spent ten months at Berlin, in order to cement (in his father's name) the union of their territory with the crown of Prussia. At the same time he became acquainted with the genial Prince Henry Radziwill, the amiable original of Goethe's Faust, whose wife, the noble Princess Louise, was sister to Prince Louis Ferdinand; and with Count Bernstorff, the companion of Gerlach, tutor to the Crown Prince of Lancizolle; and friendships were formed with them which death alone could terminate, and of which the young Countess Anna afterwards reaped the benefit.

Next to the Prince William in their circle of friends came the two ladies — his wife Marianne and the Princess Louise Radziwill, a Princess of the Prussian royal family. The Princess William resided at that time in the castle of Fischbach, among the mountains, which reminded her so much of the hills of her childhood, and was the model of a German princess as well as the model of a German wife and mother. She was full of gentleness, very courteous, very amiable, almost childlike in her simplicity, and all her actions were pervaded by an atmosphere of true piety. She knew how to adorn her home circle with the most beautiful fruits of love. "The comfort of love" was her royal nephew's name for her, on account of the truth of her friendships and her unwearying readiness to help, and she soon made the young around her acknowledge her claim to this name. Notwithstanding this, there burned a brave spirit in this woman, which was fanned by Stein's fiery eloquence, and made her long, with ever-increasing earnestness, for the deliverance of her country, and this flame was nourished by her friend the Princess Louise Radziwill until it burned very strongly indeed.

During their quiet life at Konigsberg, the

two princesses, for the first time, knew each other well, and they became the most devoted friends. Hand in hand they henceforth went on their way together, and were unwearied in caring for the wounded who had fallen in the war. They organized bands of women, and erected hospitals, and nursed and tended the sick and injured. On the day of the battle of Leipzic, the Princess William found on her steps a child three weeks' old, whose father had fallen before the enemy, and whose brother had died from grief and want. The Princess took the little orphan into her house and into her motherly heart, and in many such ways gained the love of the people, till their affection for her equalled their love for their former Queen Louise. And when the King, in remembrance of this dear departed one, instituted the Louise Order, as an acknowledgment of the labours of love of these ladies during the war, the two princesses were the first whom he decorated with his own hands, at the same time placing the Princess William at the head of the whole order.

Right worthily after these women comes the grey-headed field-marshal Gneisenau, who, in the even-time of a life rich in summer sunshine, so peacefully rested in the beautiful Erdmannsdorf, decorated by the laurels he had won in the war for freedom. He entered into the closest friendship with Prince William and Count Anton, particularly as they had been fellow-soldiers with Blücher and Grohnann, Boyen Groben, and Roder.

Another who joined very harmoniously in this circle of friends was the pious Countess Reden. Her castle of Buchwald had long been a central point for the circulation of the Bible and the spread of missions. Champions of the pure scriptural faith were found there from all parts of Germany and England, some of them members of the Established Church, and some members of the quiet Moravian congregations. As early as 1808, Stein, "the political Luther," as Arndt calls his friend, returned from his flight to Bohemia to Buchwald, and the faith which he had inherited from his mother found fresh strengthening there. And now, in the evening of his life, old Stein came back over the Rhine into the quiet valley of the Riesengebirge, and to the noble men with whom he had passed such a weighty time. There he was often led to the top of the Falkenstein, which had been adorned by the Princess William and her children, Adelbert and Waldemar, Elizabeth and Marie, with a large iron cross on their father's birthday. It bore the inscription, "May the blessing of the Cross rest on William, his friends, and the whole valley!" And the children would sit there listening with sparkling eyes as their elders spoke of the bygone days they had spent together, and told of the fathers who had watered the seemingly dead tree of Germany with their hearts' blood, and of the mothers who had bound up their wounds, and they resolved to follow their example, and to win, too, the Iron Cross or the Louise Order. But far different impressions fell from the circle of parents on the tender heart of the little Anna Stolberg; faith in God, love for her fatherland, reverence for the King, love to her neighbours, were the lessons she learned.

CHAPTER V.

COLOGNE — DIERSFORDT — KREPPEL — DUSSELDORF — MAGDEBURG.

"And the seed should spring and grow up, he knoweth not how."—MARK iv. 27.

THE year 1830 scattered the friendly circle on the Falkenstein. Prince William went to Cologne as Governor of the Rhineland and Westphalia, and again Anton Stolberg accompanied him as adjutant, this time, however, with a pen instead of a sword. His wife and his ten blooming children went with him. Two had been taken away by death from the parent home, the four-year-old Elizabeth at Peterswaldau, and the five-year-old Udo three years before at Kreppelhof.

The next year the old Gneisenau was summoned to the armies above. The invincible hero of the battle-field was struck down by cholera at Posen.

Already the aged Stein was praying in his home at Kappenberg, in Westphalia :—

> "Oh, make my bed so soft, so smooth,
> For I am weary, and must sleep!"

Very soon afterwards he lay ready to sleep, and as his failing sight fell on a picture which hung over his bed (the portrait of his deceased wife), he had it brought to him, and wrote in large letters on the frame, "Christ is my life, and death my victory."

When in the lovely summer days his funeral proceeded along the Rhine to the burying-place of the old counts, it was as if it had been the burial of a king From every church tower the mourning bells tolled, and from village to village, from town to town, the people followed the dead hero. These mourning bells were heard in Count Anton's house, and the children wept for the old friend of their childhood, whom they had hugged and kissed but one year before in their Silesian home. So one day their father took them to the high tower in Nassau which Stein had himself built, and showed them precious relics of the fatherland which the Prussian regenerator had gathered in troubled yet glorious times. The memories of Stein were the memories of Count Anton Stolberg too. "Germany! Germany before all else!" cried every picture, every sword, every pen to the children. And their father told them how Stein had hoped much more for his cause from German spirit than from German swords; and how his great desire had been to strengthen the minds of the German youth. Then they descended from Stein's tower to Stein's grave in the family burial-place at Fürth, and read the inscription: "Humble before God, noble towards men; an enemy of lies and falsehood, devoted to duty and fidelity, unmoved by contumely or persecution; the uncrushed son of crushed Germany; the deliverer of his country in battle and victory." And then over all stood out the longing of the Christian: "I have a desire to depart and to be with Christ."

Such a scene as this remained indelibly impressed on the young Countess Anna. These hours lay like a fructifying cloud of dew on the spring ground of her heart, and the seed was nourished by them.

In 1831 Count Anton Stolberg inherited from his brother-in-law the beautiful territory of Diersfordt. Here the family lived till the autumn of the following year, returning to Kreppelhof in the spring of 1834, back to their Silesian friends.

The former activity of the Count as Royal

Commissioner in the Rhenish Provinces at Düsseldorf was the cause of his appointment to be president of that town. For three long years he worked there with the same self-sacrifice and the same blessing as in his previous position as landlord in his country home, and was rewarded by the same love and gratitude. His children continued to bloom, and freshly and brightly did they cluster in the summer months in the castle of Düsseldorf.

This three years' residence by the lovely Rhine was very important with regard to the mental and inner development of the young Countess Anna. Many men celebrated in the religious or political world, or in art or science, visited the hospitable home of the President. The Count Frank Joseph Spee, Metternich zur Grailt, Von der Recke, and Baron von Hymmen, with many other notable members of the Rhenish nobility, rallied round the Count's house. And among these highborn nobles sat two men ennobled by wisdom, William Schadow, the nephew of a poor Berlin tailor, yet the great artist and director of the Berlin Academy, and father of a new school of painting, and Felix Mendelssohn Bartholdy, the son of a Jew, the then young master of music. Count Anton frequently took his children to Schadow's studio, and drew lessons for himself and them from the great oil painting, " The Wise and the Foolish Virgins," which the artist was at that time finishing.

He listened with the greatest delight to the soul-inspiriting playing of Felix Mendelssohn, and he and his family neglected none of the great Rhenish musical festivals which this composer knew so well how to create and conduct. When the young master used to improvise on the piano by an open window on a summer's evening, the President and his daughters might have been seen walking up and down before his dwelling for hours, listening to the wonderful sounds. "I never heard such heavenly music as in the Düsseldorf streets under his window," remarked the Countess Anna, many years afterwards. She preserved this same intense, fresh joy in what was pleasant all through the heaviest work of her future calling, and great was the blessing it proved to her.

The chief and most abiding influence, however, which fell on the whole course of our Anna's life, arose from her father's intimacy with Pastor Fliedner of Kaiserswerth—an intimacy which was formed at this time and continued during the remainder of the two men's lives.

Theodore Fliedner's activity in his small and poor congregation is well known. Its very continuance was due to his unwearying zeal. In the collecting journeys which he made through the Rhine Provinces, Holland, and England, quite new ideas about his home work came before his mind, and through Elizabeth Fry he felt constrained to take an interest in the prisoners on his return to Düsseldorf. After conquering great difficulties he and some other Evangelical Christians formed in 1826 the first German Prisoners' Society in Rhenish Westphalia. The members set themselves the important and difficult tasks of placing clergymen and schoolmasters in the Rhine Provinces, of dividing the prisoners into classes according to their age and the nature of their offence, and of giving them work and providing for their welfare at the expiration of their punishment. And God gave his blessing to this work of love.

Soon afterwards Fliedner commenced his "Women's Society for the Employment of Prisoners," and after another journey, during which he improved his acquaintance with Elizabeth Fry, he established the asylum for discharged female prisoners at Kaiserswerth.

On the 17th September, 1833, Fliedner received the first woman into his tiny gardenhouse, without dreaming that from this small beginning so many establishments of blessing would arise.

About this time Count Spee, the President of the Prussian Committee, introduced Fliedner to the Stolbergs at Düsseldorf, and he soon became one of their dearest guests. Count Anton sympathized with all his heart and with zealous help in the work of the society. In 1835 the Kaiserswerth pastor helped the Düsseldorf president to form the first infant school in that town, and the Countess and her daughters took the most lively interest in the juvenile establishment. The Count and Fliedner had many an earnest conversation about the need of their brethren and about the

Christian duty of helping the poor and sick, the miserable and forsaken, and so they gradually began to talk about the work of "deaconesses." "Ought not our Evangelical Christian women," Fliedner used to ask, "to be able and willing to help to nurse the sick? Did not the Apostolic Church employ their powers in behalf of the suffering members of their body, and were there not official deaconesses for many centuries? Why should we delay longer in restoring this office to the handmaidens of the Lord?" These conversations were often drunk in by two glistening eyes, sometimes nearly overflowing with tears, and then Fliedner, with his love for the young, used lovingly to stroke the fair girl's head. Did he guess that in the young Anna Stolberg his most devoted and faithful candidate for the deaconess service stood before him? Perhaps not; but one day he was to find it out.

They did not remain long satisfied with

talking, deeds rapidly followed. On the 30th of May, 1836, the regulations for the Deaconesses' Society of Rhenish Westphalia were signed in Count Anton's house at Düsseldorf. He was chosen president of the society, which was placed by Fliedner in connection with the provincial synods of the Rhine and Westphalia, and the object of the institution was announced to be the training of evangelical nurses for the sick.

"With God's help all things are possible!" Strengthened by this motto of faith, Fliedner set busily to work, and on Oct. 13th, 1836, the deaconess establishment and hospital of Kaiserswerth were opened. The commencement was discouragingly small. The deaconess house began without any deaconesses, and the hospital without any patients. Besides this, the accommodation was of the poorest. At last the first inmate arrived. The daughter of a physician was the first deaconess, and a

Catholic girl from Kaiserswerth the first patient.

But the gardener looked trustingly up to heaven, and so God gave the rain and sunshine, and out of the tiny seed on the Rhine there grew a giant tree, whose branches soon spread over the whole earth.

It was a great treat to Anna to visit Kaiserswerth with her parents and sisters, and with her hand in Fliedner's to be led through his young establishment. This pleasure was frequently repeated, for the president of the Deaconess Society performed no mere nominal duty; his strong interest in the cause took him almost weekly to the Kaiserswerth institution. It flourished wonderfully. From the little room in the garden-house of the parsonage, the first asylum of discharged female prisoners, grew a Magdelene Asylum; from the knitting and infant school a training school for teachers, and to this was soon added a home for orphan girls. And this was all watched by the quiet, thoughtful eyes of the young Countess; she saw the planting, the growing, the flourishing of the work, and marked in surprise how "the father of the deaconesses" was continually calling forth more and more women to the help of their suffering brethren, and the impressions she then received were not forgotten by her.

Besides this, Count Anton and his family used to be much interested in going to Düsselthal, to visit the institution for girls founded by one of his great friends, the Count von der Recke.

In 1836 Anna was confirmed in the parish church of Diersfordt. During the preparation for the confirmation, this young Christian was, for the first time, heavily burdened by a sense of her great sinfulness; but she cried with strong tears, "I cannot let thee go except thou bless me," until at last the Lord gave her the precious blessing of realising his promise, "Though your sins be as scarlet, they shall be white as snow." Then her delivered soul jumped for joy. The sower does not always sow all his seed at once. He sows here and there, early and late, and then waits for the various harvest-times. So while the first spring seeds had already begun to flower beautifully in Anna's heart, new germs were at this season planted there, and in the midst of many tears and God's sunshine they sprang up in due time.

Love for God—love for her neighbours—such were the seeds; a wide, wide circle reaped the rich harvest from them.

How melancholy would she have found the three following years after this busy life on the Rhine, when she had to be within the dull walls of Konigsberg, whither her father removed in the autumn of 1837 as President of the Province of Saxony, if there had not been an ever-increasing freshness in her soul, and an ever-growing devotedness and holiness!

Her father was more occupied than formerly by the great responsibilities to which he gave himself up cheerfully and unweariedly. The greatest sacrifice that his new duties entailed was the shortness of the time he could now spend in his domestic circle; but, as some compensation for the forsaken banks of the Rhine and the quiet home in Silesia, Count Anton gave his children a summer expedition from the darkness of the Magdeburg fortress to the green Harz mountains, to the village of Stolberg Wernigerode, where their uncle Henry resided. The Count Henry was married to a sister of their mother, the Countess Eberhardine, while the third brother, Count Constantin, had taken as his bride the third Mademoiselle Von der Recke.

Though now removed to a distance, Count Anton and his family always kept up their friendship with Fliedner; and Anna diligently read the yearly reports which told of the progress and development of his institutions, and was also much interested in the account given by Amelia Sieveking of the duties of the Hamburg sisters. So deeper and stronger did the love of her poor wandering brethren strike root in her heart.

CHAPTER VI.

BERLIN.

*" The river of God is full of water."—*PSALM lxv. 9.

"MY time in inquietude—my hope in God!" Such are the words on the statue of King Frederick William III. In 1840 God called his true servant from his king's purple and from his unquiet times.

" After such a father, such a son is, indeed, a gift from the Lord!" wrote the Princess William when Frederick William IV. ascended the throne. This pious king, who wrote in golden letters over the threshold of his castle, " As for me and my house, we will serve the Lord!" had a very faithful heart for his friends, and pre-eminent among these friends was Count Anton of Stolberg. It was a friendship, or rather a brotherhood, springing from their one common faith. Only death could loose such a union of hearts. As a boy the Crown Prince had loved the young lieutenant, Count Anton, whom his father and mother so highly esteemed; for during the dark year 1807 he had been at Konigsberg in attendance on the Queen Louisa. There Count Anton had watched her forbearance and humility in trial. "As God wills—just as He wills!" were her daily words during the sorrowful months of her troubles. He heard the royal hero-mother exhort her children to be men! He used to accompany "the mother of her country" to the beds of the sick and wounded soldiers, and in her visits to the schools and orphanages. He used to share with her children the instructions of the learned Madame Krudener, the pious Schaffner, and the court preacher,

Barowsky. And at this time the seed sown by God ripened in the hearts both of the Prince and the Count.

During the Count's ten months' residence in Berlin in 1822, and during the visits of the Crown Prince to Silesia and the Rhine, this friendship increased and strengthened; so one of the first acts of Frederick William IV. was to summon his " dear Anton," as he called his faithful adherent in his private circle, to his immediate presence in Berlin. Accordingly, in the beginning of 1841, Count Anton Stolberg entered on his office in the King's household. He was soon after appointed commander of the 27th Landwehr regiment, which was a peculiar gratification to him, as it was chiefly composed of men from his own province and the Wernigerode territory. In 1842 he became Minister of State, and then leader of the King's Privy Council. Earnestly desiring to serve his Sovereign, the Count took a most warm and devoted share in all the affairs of the Government, and the many efforts made by this pious king for God's glory prospered well in the hands of one so anxious about them, and so unwearied in attending to home and foreign missions, the creation of churches and schools, and countless other benevolent plans and institutions.

A new world opened in Berlin before the eyes of our young Anna—a world of glitter and festivity, but a world which neither blinded nor dazzled her simple, child-like mind. She had been accustomed to gaze at another kind of life, beautified by a more imperishable beauty than could be found in the glittering, sparkling froth of earth. So only so far as the high position of her father demanded, did either she or her mother take part in the bustling life of the court and the residence, and their hearts remained as peaceful and fresh as ever.

"The river of God is full of water." This word from the Psalms was a great help to Anna in the dried-up atmosphere of Berlin society.

Then, too, the evenings spent round the tea-table of the King and his Queen, Elizabeth, in the domestic party at Sans Souci and Charlottenburg, were very refreshing, from the high gifts and cultivation of those who composed the circle that met there; and, besides this, her parents' intercourse with the Prince and Princess William was most beneficial to our Anna! In the Berlin churches, Gossner and Heremin, Strauss and Ehrenberg, preached God's truth purely and clearly, and she sat with great interest at their feet. She often met the most earnest workers in the Lord's vineyard at the palace, as well as at the Princess William's and in her own father's house, and his position and activity brought her into connection with all the benevolent societies and institutions in Berlin.

Old "Father Gossner" had been a friend of the Stolbergs from the time when the happy, holy circle used to gather so lovingly round the snowy mountains down in their loved Silesia. In 1826 he had fled as a fugitive to the peaceful valley of the Riesengebirge to be among his "dear mountaineers," as he liked to call his friends there. His dear mountaineers remained bound for life to him. It was to their intercession with Frederick William III., and to the zealous intervention of Baron von Kottwitz in the Consistory, that he owed the fulfilment of his earnest desire for a pulpit from which he might openly proclaim God, a desire for which he had craved during long years of waiting. He became preacher to the Bethlehem Church of the Moravian congregation at Berlin in 1829.

How delighted Count Anton and his family were the first time they saw him in his pulpit, and listened to the wonderful preacher of re-

Anna, Countess of Stolberg. 77

pentance, with his soft, moving voice (which seldom missed its way to the heart) urging the one thing needful over and over again; and then to the powerful man of prayer, with his mild, clear eyes, and his dear, quiet face, radiant with the peace of God!

Truly Gossner's power in prayer wrought wonders in Berlin. By it arose in 1833 the first band of women whose members, following Amelia Sieveking's example, devoted themselves to nursing and comforting sick women in their own houses. Then, after some years, the walls of the Elizabeth Hospital arose, in which devoted and faithful nurses ministered with the love which they had themselves received. He called into life, too, the first infant school and the Home Mission in Berlin, and established the Gossner missions in Australia, the East Indies, and the South Sea Islands.

From the praying Gossner, Anna received

very great blessing; she had been a frequent object of his petitions. She found, too, great help and blessing for her young faith in the monthly prayer-meetings of the Ladies' Nursing Society, and she used to help them as much as she could.

Pastor Gossner continued in the closest intimacy with the Count Anton Stolberg and the Princess William, and earnestly watched over their spiritual welfare. Many a quiet evening hour did they assemble in both houses, a little circle of believers round the holy man of God. After a short prayer, Gossner used to open his Bible and read a chapter, and then he used to talk about it, sometimes for an hour at a time, in the fulness of the spirit. Anna learned not only faith but humility from the old Father Gossner, with his gentle, patient, happy heart.

He desired for his nursing house no earthly riches, only just what would maintain it.

When men wished to praise the abundant fruit of his work in God's vineyard, He used to say, very simply, "We should not praise the wretched tool, but the Master; He alone has done it, and to me there remains nothing but shame and confusion for all my unfaithfulness, negligence, and sin."

Soon after the removal to Berlin, Anna formed a nearer acquaintance with a wonderful woman, a most honoured worker in the kingdom of God. One evening in the circle at the palace she saw, for the first time, England's female prisoners' apostle, Elizabeth Fry, and from that time she was often in the houses of the Princess William and of Count Anton. It was a strange, imposing, and yet home-like appearance that this woman of sixty presented in her narrow, plain, slate-coloured dress, with her fair hair covered by a Quaker cap, her fine old face looking so peaceful and gentle, her glad child-like eyes so penetratingly wise, and her friendly lips addressing the hearty "thou" of the Quakeress alike to high and low. She sat between the Queen and the Princess William on the sofa talking quite unreservedly, and telling with marvellous energy of mind, and in the most forcible language, of the physical and mental need of the poor prisoners and deserted children and unsheltered wanderers, and then she entreated and pleaded and prayed for them.

On her journey through the prisons of France, Savoy, Switzerland, and Germany in 1840, Elizabeth Fry had visited Berlin, and had, by means of Tholuck as an interpreter, spoken before a large and brilliant assembly about the improvement of prisons, exciting the greatest sympathy on all sides, and the King had then begged her to revisit the capital the next year.

How the great brown girl eyes, which had

already so thoughtfully drunk in Fliedner's and Gossner's words, lighted up when listening to Elizabeth Fry! Anna Stolberg sat quite quietly and silently in the royal circle, but her eyes spoke for her. The picture of that powerfully practical Quakeress never vanished again from her mind, and her address to the women and maidens of Germany (written at Bunsen's request) was never forgotten by her.

By desire of the King, Fliedner frequently came to Berlin now to assist Frederick William IV. in carrying out a most favourite scheme. As Crown Prince he had visited Fliedner's institution at Kaiserswerth, had informed himself thoroughly about the deaconess plan, and had supported and helped it most generously.

Immediately after his accession, he wished that his more immediate neighbourhood should share in the blessings of the deaconess work. Queen Elizabeth and the Princess William sympathized most warmly in this desire; so, under the protection of these two ladies, Fliedner brought his first five deaconesses to Berlin, on June 15th, 1843, for their happy yet heavy labour of love among the daughters of grievous sin. But the royal hearts were not satisfied even by this, they wanted to see an evangelical sisterhood firmly rooted for all time in the soil of the capital. Accordingly, the King and his Consort, the Princess William, Counts Stolberg, Von Thiele, and Eichhorn, had many consultations with Fliedner, till the plan was settled to erect in Berlin, after the pattern of the institution at Kaiserswerth, a hospital and an independent deaconess mother-house, that should gather its sisters chiefly from the eastern provinces of Prussia. In this conference and in his quiet walks with Fliedner and his dear Anton in the gardens of Sans Souci and

Charlottenburg, the King developed such generous ideas for the maintenance of his institution, that the good Fliedner looked at him with eyes of astonished reverence, and said smilingly, "Only you must always begin with a seed, your Majesty; our God never failed to give Father Gossner and me great blessing in such commencements."

"Well, dear Fliedner, what kind of seedling then do you propose I must put in the ground, that a tree may quickly grow up to answer in some measure to my expectations?"

"Oh, your Majesty, to begin with—" and he named a sum.

"Ah, ah! my dear pastor," replied the King heartily, "you good servant of poverty have no bad idea of a seedling; believe me, such a seedling is in the eyes of a King of Prussia already an established tree; we will try by God's help to plant it."

Fliedner was consequently requested to

take part in a cabinet council that the King held about the founding and establishing of the institution, so that they might benefit by his experience. The King wanted him to live half of each year in Berlin, so as to be able to manage the establishments of Kaiserswerth and Bethany too, but the modest man gratefully declined this honourable invitation, for he dreaded nothing more than divided and consequently inefficient service. Persius drew up the building plans of Bethany, and the King added to it many original and good suggestions; Stüler completed the edifice.

* * * * *

In 1844, soon after the King, amid the warmest interest of the whole Stolberg family, had laid the foundation stone of Bethany, Anna's sister, Marianne, departed joyfully to her heavenly home. This unexpected death made a great impression on her. She used afterwards to refer to the hours spent by the dying bed of her sister as the time when God wrote on her heart for her abiding peace the words, "The blood of Jesus Christ, his Son, cleanseth from all sin." This text became henceforward the motto of her life, and is now engraved on her tombstone.

Two years afterwards she stood again by a loved deathbed. Surrounded by the prayers of Gossner and of all her dearest ones, the Princess William went home to God in Easter week, 1846. The noble Princess had not been permitted to live till the consecration of Bethany, at whose foundation she had taken such an active part, for it was on the 10th of October, 1847, that it first opened its doors to the sick poor. That was a memorable ceremony never to be forgotten by our Anna. The King, the Queen, and the whole court were present. Fliedner brought over nine of his Kaiserswerth deaconesses and the superintendent Marianne von Rantzen to it. For several years the latter had devoted herself with much blessing to the heaviest toil in sick nursing, and other branches of Christian love and work. She had then diligently prepared herself for her new calling as the mother of the Berlin deaconess house, by a course of training in the Paris and Kaiserswerth hospitals. Three young probationers entered Bethany at the same time. Fliedner closed the dedication with an address and prayer. With deep emotion the King said to him, "This is a triumphant day for the Evangelical Church. May the words which the Holy Ghost spoke by your mouth receive their fullest performance." And they have received a wonderful performance.

The Countess Anna and her sisters took the deepest interest in visiting Bethany. The "mother," already a dear friend of their parents, became a truly motherly friend to the girls. They used to accompany her through the large hospital with its model accommodations so worthy of the large royal heart of Frederick William IV.; and by the beds of the sick, and watching the quiet humble labours of the "mother" and her deaconesses and probationers, the pitying love for the suffering grew rapidly in the heart of the young Countess. She used to practise sick nursing herself, without, however, dreaming how soon she would have abundant opportunity for the exercise of her newly-acquired power in her dear home in the Silesian mountains.

CHAPTER VII.

BERLIN—WERNIGERODE—KREPPELHOF.

"And after the wind an earthquake; and after the earthquake a fire; and after the fire a still small voice."—
1 KINGS xix. 11, 12.

THE stormy year 1848 brought many changes and trials to the house of Stolberg.

In Upper Silesia famine fever broke out. Immediately the King sent Count Stolberg with the most ample authority and provisions as commissioner to the sorely tried province. He arrived on February 14th, 1848, at his second home; but when, after some weeks of unwearied and most blessed labour, he returned to the King, he found Berlin changed in a most unexpected manner.

The March revolution obliged him and the whole ministry to resign, but Frederick William summoned him to the palace and at once appointed him adjutant-general. When the Count for the last time returned home from his King to the large quiet house in the Wilhelmstrasse, he found his youngest daughter, Fredericka, in a raging fever. The terrors of the past few days had tried her greatly and had thrown her on her deathbed.

The coffin of the daughter was soon to stand where the cradle of the father had stood. Her parents carried her from Berlin to their old home of Stolberg Wernigerode, and too soon, on March 27th, she fell a victim to the fever. When the Count had laid his precious child to sleep in the cool earth of the little graveyard of St. Theobald's Church, he returned with his family to the castle of Kreppelhof.

Time had caused the house once so rich and joyous with children to be very quiet and lonely now. Three daughters and one son had been carried away by death; the eldest daughter, the Countess Jenny, had been married ten years before to Count Keller; the four sons were either in State appointments or in the army; and so in the parent house there remained only the Countesses Bertha, Anna, and Charlotte. But the smaller the chain the closer will it bind the few it encloses, and in this close bond of love, amidst the peaceful solitude of the Riesengebirge, and in constant working for others, the wounded hearts began to heal. There certainly was much, very much, to do in the huts of the poor and by the beds of the sick. The distress of the previous year and of the famine fever still pressed heavily on the poor weavers of the Riesengebirge. The evangelical girls' orphanage at Altorf, which had been founded by Count Frederick zu Stolberg and his wife at Peterswaldau, and which the Rhenish Westphalian deaconesses had adopted as their first daughter-institution, could not contain all the poor girls who were desirous of being trained there as servants by six of the sisters. To alleviate the misery, Count Anton and his family exerted themselves beyond their strength. He built a little "Bethany" for the sick poor in his village of Leppersdorf, between the castle of Kreppelhof and Laudeshut. In memory of his early deceased daughter, who had taken such a heartfelt interest in the founding of Bethany, he called his hospital the Marianne Institution. His daughters helped to build it by the work of their hands. There sat the young countesses with their mother, day after day, working at a splendid large carpet. Its sale brought a rich return. This was expended by Anna and her sisters on the interior furnishing and adorning of the Marianne house. Then they seized their needles again, and made clothes and house linen, and curtains and mattresses for the institution. When it was opened to the sick women and children, the Countesses Bertha, Anna, and Charlotte served like deaconesses in their loving humility by the sick beds. But theirs was not merely a Martha activity, busy about many things, a Mary-like spirit sat too by the couches in little Bethany. And with the sickness of the body, night vanished too from many a darkened soul.

In 1850 the Countess Charlotte left her home with her parents' blessing. Following the earnest desire of her heart she entered Bethany as a sister. She wished to become trained and skilful there, and then to return as a deaconess to the Marianne Institution.

But before she could receive the consecration of the Church to this service of love she received another call. On July 24th, 1851, she gave her hand to the President of the Rhine Province of Kleist-Retzow, and accompanied him to Coblenz.

The sisters Bertha and Anna had had their minds long directed too to Bethany, and longed to enter this haven of peace, but the secession of Charlotte from the deaconess service made them hesitate to express their wish to their parents.

In the meantime Count Anton was watching with keen interest the course of events from his mountain home; he fully expected that the storm would cease and the clouds of trouble would roll away, so he went on working ceaselessly for his King in his retirement, and hoped for a better time. When his eldest son, Count Eberhard, Landrath of the circle of Laudeshut, in which place his father had begun his statesman career, was selected in 1849 from his companions for a more distinguished position, and the desire was expressed to see the administration of the magistracy once more in the old Count Anton Stolberg's hands, the grey-headed Minister of State was not too dignified to take his son's place during the whole session of seven months, acting with the same German zeal and heartiness in the modest office of a Landrath.

The stir of 1850 called the Lieutenant-General Count Anton Stolberg back to active service as adjutant-general, and brought him again to the King's side. His monarch celebrated the joyful yet sorrowful meeting by confiding to him again his favourite 27th Landwehr regiment, which had been torn from him by the storms of the revolution.

The Count was only able to return for a short time to the quiet happiness of his little family circle at Kreppelhof. The next year the King appointed him Minister of the Palace and Privy Councillor, the highest court and civil positions in Prussia, and summoned him to his immediate presence, though it was very trying to all, and especially to the daughters, to bid farewell to the Marianne house which had been adopted as a branch by the mother house of Bethany at the King's request. Since then Count Eberhard zu Stolberg has enlarged his father's work, and has added a wing for men to those for women and children.

CHAPTER VIII.

SISTER ANNA AT BETHANY.

" The fields are white already to harvest."—JOHN iv. 35.

ONCE more death entered the family circle and broke away a fresh green bough. On his return from the festival at Hohenzollern, where the King had decorated him with the Black Eagle, and had bestowed high official honours on him, Count Anton received tidings of sorrow at Prague; his second son Conrad, a happy husband and father, had suddenly gone home in the pride of his youth. Each blow made the peace of God reign the more powerfully in the hearts of the survivors.

Anna, Countess of Stolberg.

When the idle noise of the Berlin world became too much for them, the sisters Anna and Bertha knew of a refuge where they could find the quiet they had had in their Marianne Home. Often, but especially on each Sunday, they went out to the great house with the clear-sounding bell between the towers, to enjoy the favourite hymns of the sisters in that house of God, to visit the sick beds of the women and children, and to rest on the loving heart of the mother Marianne.

With what pleasure did they sing with the sisters on these Sabbath evenings the hymns of their true old friend on the Rhine, which had been introduced into Bethany by the first deaconesses from Kaiserswerth! About these days Anna afterwards wrote: "I never was so happy as at Bethany, so I went there as often as I could. Very soon a longing desire awoke in me to serve the

Lord's sick members in company with these dear sisters, and every thought about it turned to the prayer that the Lord would open my way to it. I waited patiently, and in full confidence, for the moment when He would show me by circumstances that I might speak to my dear parents about it; and sooner than I had hoped the merciful and faithful Lord heard my petition, and inclined the hearts of my parents to give me their cordial approval and blessing on October 18th, 1852."

This day was never forgotten by her to the end of her life. She celebrated it each year like a birthday, with praise and thankfulness to God and her dear parents. Both the sisters could not go; this Bertha and Anna knew. They were the last daughters, and their parents were ageing, and might soon, perhaps, require a similar ministry of love by their sick beds; so the younger sister

Anna was consecrated to the service among the poor brethren, and her father and mother conducted her themselves to the house of mercy and self-denial on June 3rd, 1853. On this day Anna received from her father her first watch, as all in that great populous building must be punctual to the minute, and every deaconess wears one. Thus simply began and ended the education of our Anna in her own home.

Scarcely a quarter of a room could the young probationer, the daughter of a distinguished nobleman, henceforth call her own— her resting place. Not even a tiny chamber, only one of the compartments ranged round the walls of the large probationers' ward. White curtains walled in the little territory, that had hardly space for a pine bedstead with green and white striped hangings, a chair, and a table. The mistress of the probationers slept with them, as she superintended their general duties and their training in sick nursing. And here the high-born countess slept next the daughter of a poor day labourer, for perfect equality in Christ was the principle carried out.

As early as half-past five the bell called Anna from her hard couch. She had barely time for her simple toilette and for the arranging of her tiny compartment before proceeding to the frugal breakfast in the hall; then came prayers in the church, and then the day's work begins. The three sisters who had the night-watch in the house give up their wards and explain their reports to their successors; these repeat it to the superintendent.

There are rooms for children, women, and men. These are separated in different ways, and accommodate both in-door and out-door patients. The head sister in each ward reads short prayers to her patients; during the day the deaconesses only read to patients by their express desire, and only pray with any weary souls who may seem to long to hear again the forgotten words of childhood after long sad struggles with sin. Every deaconess well knows that in this house of sickness her chief business is to exercise skilful hands in nursing the sick bodies; for the souls there is the pastor. Then the new probationer is led to the children's wards. This is a welcome post to Anna, with her joyful, loving, child-like heart. The children's ward continued to the end to be her favourite refreshment under the heavy trials of her position.

Bed after bed stands round the walls of the wide, airy, light rooms. Here lies a poor baby whose mother died here in giving it birth. There is great room for a work of love there; it must be cleaned, bathed, fed, quieted, hushed to sleep. There lies a girl with large tear-filled eyes; the child has broken her leg in playing. The bandages must be changed; it is true Sister Anna's hand trembles a little, for the child twitches painfully, but love makes her skilful. Here is a loathsome sore to be dressed; love conquers the disgust. There a child is crying for its mother; love suggests the best way to comfort it.

The beds have all been visited, now the room must be cleaned. Joyfully do the tender and really beautiful hands of the Countess perform the work of a servant. Certainly her unaccustomed hand does not at first understand the scouring and dusting, nor how to make the locks and bolts still brighter, nor how to polish the shining windows, but the tender fingers are wonderfully successful.

Now the room is all clean and tidy, the air pure and refreshing, so has Sister Anna time to rest? No; the whole day is busy here.

The children who are recovering want to be taught by their "dear aunt" how to play on the floor, or by the little tables with the pretty playthings so lavishly scattered in each children's ward. "Dear aunt, the wheel has come off my waggon!" "Aunt, please tie a string to my horse!" "Aunt, tell me the story of little David and the bad giant again!" "Please, please sing the hymn, 'If I am Jesu's little lamb!'" "Aunt, it hurts me here!" "Aunt, I am hungry; no, I am thirsty!" So it goes on the live-long day. Yet love is unwearying. School time has come! Like a child Anna sits with the other probationers on the narrow wooden bench, thankfully listening to the religious teaching which the house chaplain gives daily. The sisters who in their youth have only had a poor education are then helped in many branches by the teachers of the institution.

How quickly time flies in work! Midday

has come already. It is no easy work for the sisters to give each of these hundreds of invalids food, and to attend to the dietary which the doctors have specified for every patient in the five distinct divisions of the house. For the poorest patient in the gratuitous ward no wine is too costly, no game too rare, if the doctor has ordered it; that is the only limit in Bethany.

When all the sick have been attended to, the sisters meet in the hall at a general, modest midday meal. The chair of the house mother is empty. Marianne von Rantzen has been confined for many a long month to her couch of pain. On the right of the empty chair at the head of the long table sits the assistant superintendent and asks the blessing. The sisters are arranged according to their deaconess age. Sister Anna as the youngest probationer ends the row. In the afternoon more work has to be done by the sick beds, and this goes on till evening. After supper one of the elder sisters in turn reads prayers. Then the patients are washed again and are laid to rest with a short word of comfort. Thus one day after another glided swiftly away in the fulness of their occupation, rich in blessing and bright with happiness, and the Sundays with their two services were still more calm and peaceful.

From her dear children Anna was removed as a probationer to the women's wards. There was much here again that was new, and difficult to learn and conquer. Yet she worked and learned and conquered all, with holy earnestness and a strong, humble heart, for she gave herself with her whole strength to her difficult task.

A poor lost woman blasphemes God in wild jokes, cursing herself and all the world. Surely the young sister Anna will turn away full of horror and indignation! No! love keeps her near the poor sinner, love teaches her to find the right balm for the healing of this sorely wounded soul. Then, for the first time, she had to be present at a serious operation to a patient, and had to stand with the superintendent sister ready to help the doctor and the hospital deaconess. How her heart bled for the pain of the sufferer! Her blood froze in her veins and her head swam as she saw the knife work into the quivering flesh; but love strengthened her.

Here comes death with all its terrors to a bed; the sick one cannot die, will not die; the sins of her past life stand like a frightful spectre between her and her going home. She grasps the air frantically, then buries her hand deep in the bed covering, as if she could thus cling to her miserable life. All is in vain! The sick one is dead. Sister Anna has closed her dimmed eyes, has folded her cold hands on her now quiet breast, has prayed by her up to the last minute. Helped by others, she carries the body to the deadroom, and washes it, and clothes it in the white burying clothes. Then the still, still form is borne out to the chapel in the garden. Love has enabled Anna to go through it all.

Once more death knocked with his hard iron hand at the heart of this much-tried young probationer. On the 11th of February, 1854, she knelt by the deathbed of the best and dearest of fathers, and was strengthened for her laborious calling by his oft reiterated blessing on it. Count Anton went home to his fathers at peace with God and the world. The old man had injured himself at Scheinbein—a gastric and nervous fever caused his death. He took an affectionate and calm farewell of his wife and of all his children who stood round his bed. He spoke clearly and firmly of his faith, and then prayed with his confessor.* After this last earthly prayer he said simply, "Take my last greeting, my last thanks to the King my master, and to the Queen." Then he lay back in his last sleep.

His mourning sovereign ordered a splendid lying-in-state for him in his house in the Wilhelmstrasse. The simple black coffin stood under cypress and orange boughs, surrounded by high silver candelabra; at the head was a crucifix, at the feet his sword, helmet, and sash. Two stools on either side of the coffin bore the insignia of the high honours and orders, both Prussian and foreign, which the great man in the coffin had borne to the last.

The highest officials, the knights of the Black Eagle, the State ministers and the generals, all assembled in that large room of death. The King, the Queen, and all the royal family stood next the relatives round

---

* Confession is practised in the Lutheran Church.

the bier, and listened to the choir as they sung, "Jesus, my confidence!" the hymn which Louise Henricke, the consort of one of the greatest of princes, composed, and all felt he had indeed received grace "to keep the faith." Long did the King and Queen kneel in silent prayer by the coffin of their dear Anton Stolberg.

Next morning, very quietly, a train decked with flowers carried back the departed one to his earthly home. In the evening the Wernigerodes received the brother of the reigning Count by torchlight, but the old Count Henry (eighty-two years of age) was himself sick unto death, and could not show to the departed the last offices of brotherly love, or even be told of his death. And from the fresh grave in which Count Anton had been placed, in the quiet little churchyard of St. Theobald's, at the foot of the Harz mountains, where they had laid him by the side of his fathers under the free sky and in the cool earth, the Stolbergs came back to another deathbed. The very next day they had to close the weary eyes of Count Henry, eyes which had gazed bravely and trustingly on many a storm in life. In Peterswaldau one brother only remained now, Count Ferdinand; a few months afterwards he too rested in the cool earth, under the open sky.

A few weeks after the death of her father the probation time of our Anna came to an end. The great earnestness and devotion which she had shown in her duties shortened the period (which was then one year, now three) during which the sisters remained as probationers. On the 18th of April, Sister Anna received her consecration as deaconess before the altar of the church in Bethany.

Her triumphant thanksgivings for this day resounded through her whole life, even to her latest breath. "Oh, may all my life be a thank-offering for such mercy! God has called me to the dear service, He will give me grace for it. Behold the handmaid of the Lord; be it unto me according to Thy word." And truly her life was a thank-offering which ended only with her death.

The deaconess Anna now shared a little room with one other sister—such a treasure after the compartment in the probationers' ward. And yet there hardly could be anything simpler than the deaconess's tiny little room. The bedstead, the chest of drawers, and the chairs were of light pine wood. The window was shaded by long white curtains, and on the window-sill bloomed friendly flowers. Over the drawers hung a little bookcase, containing the Bible and some other religious books; round it were pictures of her relations, of her church, of her father's house, or rather her father's castle. In that stately ship one of the deaconess's brothers is now sailing over distant seas; that green mound covers her father. Over the bed hangs a crucified Jesus—the sole ornament of the room—but an indescribable atmosphere of peace pervades its small, simple limits.

The superintendent, Marianne von Rantzan, still continued very ill. She had long known the great love and devotion of the Sister Anna to the deaconess service, and she soon afterwards named her as her successor. On January 5th, 1855, the noble sufferer was happily released, and the community were unanimous in selecting Anna in her place. She accepted the call humbly, almost tremblingly, for as superintendent much that was difficult and burdensome would devolve upon her. To maintain sincerely and in the fear of God the rules and principles of the house, to manage all the necessary arrangements, to set the sisters and all the household a shining example in all the virtues of the apostolic deaconess, to stand by the sick and poor and forsaken, to guide them to the true Physician and Saviour in all their distress, to live herself a life of faith and repentance, as was essential in a Christian superintendent and as she would desire to be found in the day of judgment, such were some of the duties her new position laid upon her.

CHAPTER IX.

MOTHER ANNA IN BETHANY.

" He that is chief, as he that doth serve."—LUKE xxii. 26.

ON the 2nd of February, 1855, the Countess Anna zu Stolberg Wernigerode was solemnly dedicated to her new duties by the court chaplain in the presence of the King and Queen, as they had always taken the most lively interest in the deaconess work of Anton Stolberg's daughter and in all her service of love.

She performed more than she even promised that day. Not very long ago we might have listened in that same place to the words of her fellow-worker, the house chaplain of Bethany, over her coffin: "She has exercised among us for thirteen years the duties of superintendent, with the visible blessing of the Almighty on her complete devotion to Him. We are all witnesses how fully she performed all that her vocation demanded of her. She did not lightly regard it. The foundation of her life was her humility. Though she was strong and brave, all exercise of authority was trying to her. Her delight was to go among the poor and solitary; to be obliged to order and arrange everything forced her to exercise great self-denial and self-control. And yet I have learned in her increasingly the truth of the old word, 'Who serves reigns.' Her influence was very powerful; we feel it in the gap that she has left behind her. It was because she served the Lord before all else that He so blessed her. His word was her daily bread, his church her joy, and his house the object of her desire when she was far from it. She gave her whole soul to the work appointed to her; her duty became her pleasure, and Bethany her dearest place, her home on earth, the spot which she would not leave nor have exchanged for any other."

Truly she found it no light work to be superintendent, but her strength grew wonderfully with her need. When she entered Bethany there were hardly fifty sisters; now one hundred and fifty deaconesses and probationers are working there and at the branch institutions, and every one of them turned in every difficulty of their minds or duties to their "dear mother." Thirteen years ago Bethany only counted two branch houses, the Marianne Institution at Kreppelhof and the hospital at Potsdam; now there belong to Bethany twenty-four institutions, with seventy-four sisters, all set on foot by Anna herself, and aided in their management by her practical directions. Of course she possessed a peculiar talent for organization, especially in little things; everything became straight when she took it decidedly in hand.

She had a special pleasure in sending two deaconesses to the new hospital at her birthplace, Peterswaldau, which had been founded by her cousin Count Frederick, who was also the founder of the large girls' orphanage at Altdorf.

At the same time her duties in the house were very pressing. The number of the sick beds increased from year to year. Frederick William IV. alone endowed twenty free beds, which are to this day adorned by a porcelain plate with his name and one of his favourite texts on it, and which are kept filled with poor patients by the widowed Queen. The two superintendents, Marianne and Anna, each also endowed in their lifetime a free bed. Now Bethany has nearly three hundred beds. And for all, sick and well, Mother Anna had to care, to order, to overlook; over sick wards and kitchens, over the medicines for the apothecary sister, over the bandages and charpie, over her house linen and stores (regular caskets of order and cleanliness), over the gardens and cowhouses, she reigned in her perfect gentleness.

At no important operation of the renowned Wilms did she ever fail; she and two assistant sisters always gave the necessary help and did the dressing. Only when a young assistant-surgeon in his wisdom sometimes loosened the healing dressing, to study for himself and his attendant friends "this especially interesting case," unmoved by the prolonged pain of the patient, mother Anna could not stand by patiently. Her love for her poor sick ones was the key-note of her whole life on earth!

And yet Anna's heart was not satisfied with this great and ceaseless life of activity. The wide poor neighbourhood of Bethany alone knows the whole extent of her unwearied secret self-denial. The yearly income of her private fortune was almost too small for her great heart; she frequently gave it entirely away. Even the frequent experience of having been deceived by unworthy objects could not harden her tender heart; and not only did she give with an open heart and hand, she worked also incessantly for her poor. The good sisters helped their dear mother most truly. It is not permissible, by the rules of the house, to give presents to the superintendents or to the house officials on their birthdays; but they very well knew what would give their "mother" the greatest pleasure on her birthdays; so, during the whole year, the sisters, in their few leisure moments, and by the beds of the patients, busily knitted children's socks and made clothes and aprons, and on the 6th of September each year they brought all these treasures to their dear mother with a beautiful morning hymn as an offering of love on her birthday; and shortly before Christmas many poor women used to come to Bethany to carry away winter clothing and stockings to delight their little ones at that holy time, and for each mother Anna had a true, hearty word, a friendly smile, a warm pressure of the hand. Next day, all the happy children used to come at noon in their new clothes to Bethany, and Anna and the sisters used to take the poor little ones on their laps, and kiss them, and feast them in the hall with sweet coffee and great pieces of cake, and then used to give them pretty pictures to take away with them. Day after day crowds of poor people came to be fed and nourished, yet there always remained something over, so liberally did Anna and the cooking sister provide.

Christmas Eve was a specially beautiful festival at Bethany. Through the well-lighted church resounded the songs of the sisters, pure and lovely like angels' voices. In each sick room Christmas trees blazed brightly. The children had learned Christmas hymns from the teaching sisters, and so the "mother" used to go from room to room with her sweet, tender smile, and great, happy, childlike eyes, and from bed after bed heard the old childish hymns, and then bent down and kissed each little lisping one with a true mother's heart.

Every child and every patient received a Christmas present. Each sister had made some little thing for their dear "mother," and she used to be as pleased as a child over the most simple little offering. She never forgot any sister; even for each one in the distant houses she used to fill a little bag with apples and nuts and writing paper or gloves, or a book, or a picture, just as her love suggested.

Easter was another joyful festival at Bethany. Then Anna gave the coloured eggs which her mother, or the children of her sister Jenny brought in great number, to the intense delight of the little sufferers in the wards, and then there was a special distribution in the hall for the numerous children of the house servants of coloured eggs of every shade, and chocolate, and beautiful toys. Mother Anna shared in the amusements like a child, and even the gravest sister was soon forced to enter into the happy excitement. All the little ones looked forward to this Easter festival the whole year.

Very sweet, too, were the quiet birthday evenings of "the mother," spent in the midst of some of the sisters and the most intimate of the house officials. She used to be as happy as a child, and used to tell them about the happy days of her youth in her parents' home. She had one pleasant summer week of rest from her hard work at Kreppelhof in the play-place of her childhood, in the midst of her own family and with her mother. How the old memories revived again! No one was allowed to give her presents on her birthdays, but she had instead a great surprise for her guests; now a picture of her dear children's ward, then a view of the workroom or of the beautiful church at Bethany.

This church was her great darling, to deck it her greatest pleasure. Though so particularly modest and unostentatious in her personal requirements, she could never do enough to adorn her church with beautiful gold and silver ornaments and coloured tapestries. She delighted to send such presents to the chaplain as birthday offerings. Curiously enough, as if she had had a presentiment that she would never see that day again, she sent by the sisters on her last Christmas a very beautiful gold candelabra with seven branches, formed after the model of the ancient churches, for special occasions. She had spared no trouble in sketching from old libraries the correct design for the goldsmith; she tried to have her jewel quite perfect; and soon the seven lights of the golden branches burned at the head of her own coffin!

It was a pleasant time, not only for Anna, but for all the sisters, when her mother and her sister Bertha came from Potsdam to spend some days at Bethany. They greatly enjoyed coming to this quiet home of peace. Even if they were rather crowded in the one bedroom, Anna knew how to help with a pleasant word in arranging the modest accommodation. "I learned bivouacking in Flensburg and Altona, mamma!" How the deaconesses loved the simple, affectionate, old lady and the Countess Bertha! They do so even now, when years have passed since the mother, "full of days," went home.

CHAPTER X.

SOUTH GERMANY—ALSACE—SWITZERLAND.

*"Let thine eyes be on the field that they do reap, and go thou after them."—*RUTH ii. 9.

THE revived idea of the ancient service of deaconesses spread with wonderful rapidity from Kaiserswerth over the country, and like the thousand-year-old wheat-seed from the Pyramid tombs of the Egyptian kings, the seed of love and faith sprang up and grew and ripened and bore fruit a thousandfold.

"Let me glean and gather after the reapers among the sheaves," said Ruth in the field of Boaz.

This was the feeling which induced Anna, in the summer of 1856, to start on the greatest journey of her life, and to bear the longest separation from her field of work, for she wanted to see whether among the ripe sheaves of the deaconess blessing in strange fields she might glean some new grains of corn for the field of her Bethany. And her search, like that of the industrious, faithful Ruth, was not in vain.

Accompanied by the house chaplain of Bethany, she visited not only the Protestant but also the Catholic nursing establishments of South Germany, Alsace, and Switzerland, to inquire into the minutest details of their management and to compare them with Bethany.

In Dresden the deaconess house for the kingdom of Saxony was visited, which had been founded by the noble Countess Hohenthal-Königsbrück in 1844, under the guidance of

Fliedner. She particularly enjoyed her visit to Kaiserswerth and the hours spent with Fliedner again. How much they had to talk about! How widely his field had spread since Anna had last seen him! In fifty-nine outlying stations, in America and Asia, in Jerusalem, Alexandria, and Europe, even in the proudest cities of Roman Catholicism, there were working one hundred and seventy-seven of the two hundred and fifty deaconesses that had been trained at Kaiserswerth.

At Strasburg the travellers were greatly pleased with the quiet working and joyous devotedness in the institution opened there by Pastor Härter in 1842. With this house were connected a Magdalen Asylum, a reformatory for young women prisoners after their discharge from prison, and a servant training school which was especially valued in Alsace.

The golden grain of the deaconess home at Basle was flourishing most promisingly; it had been established in 1852 by Fliedner's influence and by Spittler, the well-known founder of the Crischona Mission.

Then it was very refreshing and instructive to the travellers to converse with Pastor Germond in French Switzerland about nursing homes and the deaconess cause which lay so close to his heart, and to visit his beautifully situated little institution, established in 1842 at Echallens, and afterwards moved to St. Loup.

In Neuenburg Anna was witness to a scene of world-wide celebrity which touched her very nearly. Her father had followed with the greatest interest the conduct of the throne of Prussia to the canton of Neuenburg, which, notwithstanding the decision of all the sovereigns of Europe, refused to acknowledge the King of Prussia as its ruler. How her heart must have beat, then, when early in the morning of September 3rd she was awoke by the noise in the streets, and looking out of the window saw the black and white banner of her King waving from its old castle! The Count Pourtales Steiger and the Lieutenant Meuron had stormed the castle in the night with three hundred Royalists, and had taken possession of it for the King of Prussia as lawful ruler. But it was a short triumph, the power of the democratic party penetrated into the castle, tore down the Prussian colours, and took the Royalists prisoners. When the news of the troubles in Neuenberg, a thousandfold exaggerated, reached Berlin, the sisters at Bethany became very anxious about their dear mother; but they received a very happy letter from her from Strasburg, where she was renewing her friendship with the beloved teacher of her childhood and the faithful friend of her after life, Fraulein

Guyenet, a friendship which was afterwards still further strengthened at Bethany.

On the return journey she visited the Lutheran deaconess home in Neuendettelsau, which had been founded with many peculiar directions and perfectly independently. It was established in 1854 by Pastor Löhe, and had already spread a mighty influence over two quarters of the world.

Bethany received many a grain of corn from this diligent gleaning of its mother in strange fields, which bring forth fruit to this day.

CHAPTER XI.

ALTONA—FLENSBURG—GORLITZ.

"He bound up his wounds, pouring in oil and wine."
—LUKE x. 34.

IT was a great refreshment and help to the lady superintendent of Bethany that her work brought her into the closest connection with her eldest brother Eberhard, chancellor of the order of St. John of Jerusalem, at their common field of work by the bedside of their sick brethren.

At the commencement of our century, in the troublous times of political and religious disorder, when dynasties hundreds of years old were overthrown and shattered, an uproar arose, from want of true appreciation, against the venerable order of the Knights of St. John. The impulsive, active King, Frederick William III., could not bear any life that seemed one of mere pretence, so by a cabinet order of January 22nd, 1811, he drove the order out of his country, and seized their rich possessions to replenish his coffers, which had been emptied by the unhappy years of warfare. Merely the insignias of the order were to remain in existence, and these, like all other decorations, were to be at the King's disposal.

Frederick William IV. was not at all satisfied with this state of things. His loving heart, which beat so warmly for all the wretched and poor and needy, knew that the Knights of St. John had no mere name for brave and kindly deeds. In the autumn of 1852, on his birthday, he recalled to life the dead branch of the order. He did not help them with money or with the restoration of their property, but he gave them a more secure guarantee by restoring to them their original duties of Christian mercy to the poor and sick, of the alleviation of misery and want, of visiting the hospitals, of opposing infidelity—deeds of chivalry in the widest sense of the word, conquering the enemy, maintaining the truth, helping the wretched. And so, according to the old statutes of the Knights of Jerusalem, who delighted in their title of Hospitallers, the poor and the miserable were their sole masters.

Frederick William took great interest in the restoration of the old decaying tree. Their troubles might indeed have broken the form of the Knights of St. John, but not their spirit—the spirit of Christian piety! Like a breath of spring air the King's summons wafted over the evangelical German nobility, and noble men came in hundreds from all sides, who had long borne the sign of the cross on their hearts, and who now had the small white linen cross with the words "Pro fide" fastened on their breasts; and so fresh, joyful life again beat strongly through the old order.

Among the first knights of the restored order were Count Anton Stolberg, his sons, and all the other Stolbergs. For centuries this family had been faithful members of it, and had accompanied pilgrims on their journeys to the Sepulchre; they had clothed the naked, fed the hungry, and nursed the sick, and had transmitted the chivalrous spirit from generation to generation even in the times when the word "hospitaller" was only an empty sound. And a Stolberg was soon again to take a prominent place in the resuscitated order. The flaming zeal of the Count Eberhard zu Stolberg elevated him to be chancellor of the order, and he has been a light and a staff to it to the present day. The knights began their work full of pious joy and zeal. By their means there speedily arose in all the Prussian provinces, and even in distant lands, various hospitals; and in this blessed path of love, hospital service, we shall henceforth see Eberhard and Anna Stolberg walking hand in hand.

Whenever he built a new hospital, he immediately knocked at the doors of Bethany for help, and each time she at once set out with some deaconesses, whom she introduced to the new hospital and instructed in their necessary duties. In this way Eberhard and Anna Stolberg opened twenty-four nursing homes and hospitals in connection with his order. In the autumn of 1860, when Bethany gave up its hospital at Polzin to the knights, they made a solemn compact to manage it according to the deaconess rules, and to have all their hospitals under their superintendence. Soon afterwards Eberhard and Anna Stolberg, with their respective bands of helpers, were called to a new and extensive work of mercy.

* * * * * *

In October, 1863, there gathered at Geneva an assemblage of men with warm, loving hearts. The noble Swiss, Henry Dunant, had summoned them to consult how they could, in some measure, mitigate the frightful miseries caused by the war and the sufferings of the poor wounded—sufferings which became increasingly terrible as the weapons of destruction became increasingly powerful—by exercising the activity flowing from pitying kindness. Henry Dunant had visited the bloody field of Solferino as a simple tourist; he saw the agonies of thousands of wounded on the battle-field; he saw the shattered members bleeding because no one was near to bind them up; he saw deadly mortification seizing victims whose lives could easily have been saved by timely amputation; he saw how, in heartless, thoughtless hurry, fainting ones were thrown into graves with the dead; he saw the frightful miseries of thirst, and no one hand ready to relieve it; he saw the uninviting hospitals and ambulances with their inefficient, indifferent attendants, and thousands of wounded dying in them in speechless agony; and this cruel picture never vanished from before his eyes. Day and night he heard the cries, the moans, the shrieks, the groans of despair and death proceeding from the helpless, the wounded, the needy, and his heart bled. And ever and ever he felt forced to wonder whether there was no help on earth for this misery, for this agony, crying as it did to heaven. Then, like a ray of summer sunshine, an idea flashed upon him. He thought of the devoted women and girls of Castiglione, who had nursed the wounded soldiers, and had with tender hands bound up their wounds. He remembered how, as early as the "War of Freedom," the Sister Martha of Besançon had nursed and tended and dressed the wounded, both of the French and of the allied armies; how, in the Crimea, the Princess Helena Paulowna of Russia (née Princess Charlotte of Wurtemberg), with three hundred noble St. Petersburg ladies, had acted as loving nurses in the Russian hospitals; while at the same time in the English hospitals Miss Florence Nightingale and Miss Stanley, with eighty-seven noble Englishwomen, had nursed the sufferers of Balaclava and Inkermann. So he thought, " Can what these weak and often ignorant women can do, and are doing, be impossible to us strong, instructed, active men? But pitying love alone can constrain us, and this love must be called forth and searched after!"

This holy spark, which fell into the heart of Henry Dunant by the poor wounded at Solferino, burned on and on so strongly, that he could not rest until his ideas had grown to deeds. He wrote his book, "Recollections of Solferino," depicting the miseries of the wounded in the liveliest colours, and impressing upon the hearts of all Christians in the most earnest language the duty of caring for their brethren, and of laying the foundations in all countries during a time of peace of a band of voluntary helpers for nursing the sick and wounded in any future wars.

The call sounded powerfully to many hearts, most powerfully to the Prussian knights, the knights of the sword and of war, though they had already been led by the warlike events of 1856 and 1859 to make very extensive preparations among themselves for affording help to the sick and wounded in case of another war. Accordingly, when, at the call of Henry Dunant and General Dufour, representatives from almost all the countries of Europe assembled at Geneva on the 26th of October, 1863, "to form an international convention for the care of the sick and wounded in war," the Knights of St. John were worthily represented by Prince Henry XIII.

From that time the sufferers in battles have been well cared for. As a consequence of the Geneva Convention, a number of well-known and respected men soon gathered at Berlin to work for the wounded, high princes standing side by side with mere burghers in their zeal, and their wives not being left behind in ardour. The Knights of St. John were, however, pre-eminent in their earnestness. It seemed as if an unseen voice from above were calling, "Arise, for the time when your help will be wanted approaches fast!"

On the 1st of February, 1864, the united Prussians and Austrians passed over the Oder to free their brethren of Schleswig-Holstein from the Danish yoke. Then the "Convention" redoubled its efforts for the victims of the battles. With the hearty approval of the King and Queen, the Berlin Society formed itself into a central committee, from which offshoots were to spread over the whole country. Money and instruments, linen and provisions, were collected from all the provincial and local committees, and special attention was given to the training of male and female nurses. The Knights of St. John offered to erect hospitals at the seat of war in conjunction with the military authorities, to send to them doctors, nurses, and assistants, and to maintain them at their own expense.

Once more the chancellor of the order, to whom, in the fullest confidence, all the arrangements for the field hospitals had been left, knocked at the doors of Bethany, at the heart of his sister. "Anna, help! we need the hands of your sisters more than ever, we need yourself!" Did Anna hesitate a moment? No; quickly did she prepare, and quickly was she ready; and on January 31st, 1864, she proceeded with two deaconesses, her brother Eberhard and his wife Maria, the Count Ernest of Lippe-Weissenfels, and two brothers accustomed to sick nursing, to the Rauhe Haus, to form the first Johanniter field-hospital at Altona.

Anna, Countess of Stolberg, was the first deaconess employed in a battle-field! Fresh deaconesses followed their mother rapidly from Bethany and Kaiserswerth, and the houses both of Protestant and Catholic sisterhoods; and the Johanniter master, Count Eberhard zu Stolberg, had a constant succession of knights offering themselves as assistants. They rented at Altona a large house, with nineteen bright, airy apartments, and it was soon ready in the hands of "the mother" and her deaconesses as a pattern hospital with fifty-five beds, and was arranged for the reception of wounded or sick soldiers without distinction of rank or creed, and whether they were Prussians, Austrians, or Danes.

Over the door was exhibited the large cross of the Johanniters, and the inscription, "Hospital of the Knights of St. John," while over the house waved a white banner with a red cross. A similar cross was worn by all the Johanniters, doctors, nurses, and assistants, on a white band round their arms. As early as 1759, Frederick the Great

Anna, Countess of Stolberg. 145

acknowledged that nurses were neutral and invulnerable people in war, and since the Geneva Conference a red cross on a white ground worn round the arm, or floating on a banner over a house, is a sacred sign to all besieging armies. Hitherto, no battle had taken place. The Johanniters and the Deaconesses merely worked quietly hand in hand preparing for the coming strife.

Hark! hark! what is that dull noise resounding through the snowy winter air? What are the cries and shrieks and groans that echo so terribly between the dull thundering reports? Those are the cannons sounding so fearfully loud; these are the moans of pain, the death-cries of the poor soldiers, whose flesh has been torn by a ball, or a sabre-cut, or a bayonet. The iron hand of war stretches out its bloody finger imploringly, and beckons: "You quiet, peaceful people, help! Your brothers bleed;

come, come, bind their wounds, help the fainting!" And not in vain did the cannons call by their thunder, or the wounded moan, or the bloody finger beckon. Quickly hundreds of red crosses on a white ground appeared on the battle-field; they sprang up even in the thickest of the fight; they carried refreshment even under the firing to the warriors, and bent over the soldiers embedded in the bloody snow, and the tired, sorrowful eyes were raised hopefully to them, for the red cross said plainer than words, "Helping, brotherly love is here!" The brave bearers carried their wounded brethren in their arms out of the hot rain of shots, attending alike to the cries for help in German or Danish that sounded in their ears; for if this hand only a minute ago held the enemy's glittering sword, it belongs now to a needy brother. The white badge becomes dyed purple, the winter storm drives the biting sleet into their faces, but they do not mind. With undaunted zeal they carry their precious booty (snatched from death) through the knee-deep snow to the Rhenish company of the Johanniters and to the waggons provided by Prince Pless for the transport of the sick and furnished with comfortable spring mattresses, and these waggons convey the wounded to the specially prepared train, and so they arrive at the hospital.

Conspicuous among all the red crosses in the bloody field, there shines one on a little white linen cross surrounded by the words "Pro Fide." "Pro Fide" on their breasts, and true German pity and brotherly love in their hearts, these are the Knights of St. John, and chief among them all is their chancellor, Eberhard, Count Stolberg!

Meanwhile, Anna and her deaconesses were perfectly ready for their work in the hospital at Altona. On the 6th of February the Johanniters brought them the first wounded, eight Austrian soldiers; and then the hospital filled rapidly. The heavy work by the sick beds began; like messengers of peace the deaconesses moved about among the victims of the war, to close the wounds which the sword had opened. Night or day there was no more rest for Anna or her sisters; night and day for weeks. they hardly had their clothes off. Scarcely had they stretched their weary limbs on a straw palliasse at some late hour of the night, after a day of great labour, and drawn the woollen rug over them (for the good beds were entirely reserved for the sick), when there was another knock; it was a new arrival of wounded, and so their night's rest is gone. Over and over again they had to administer nourishment, to wash, to bind up, to comfort, till the morning light brought a new day's work; but love gave strength for all!

And this love conquered much that was more difficult to bear than work or deprivation—the scornful ingratitude of many rough soldiers, the rude insolence from men who did not understand the deaconesses' position, hitherto so unheard of in Prussian hospitals, and who would not submit to the "nuns;" but very soon the gentleness and mildness, the unwearying self-denial, the humble service of the sisters, conquered even the rough soldiers, and tamed the most determined insubordination. With something of the hopeful feeling with which they had marked the Johanniters' red cross on the battle-fields, they trustingly, respectfully, and gratefully gazed at the red cross on their nurses' arms, and at the quiet faces in the white caps. One deaconess wrote thus from a sick bedside: "Just as a child looks for its mother, and likes her best to help it, and pours out its heart to her and finds peace with her, so do our soldiers look to us!"

"But, Mother Anna, your sisters understand and speak no Danish; what will they do in nursing so many of the wounded prisoners from the enemy?"

"From the enemy! We have, we know no enemy. Love understands and speaks every language in the world!"

When the Johanniters had carried the wounded from the battle-field to the hospitals, and had buried the dead in the bloody earth, they resumed their work as "Hospitallers." They attended to all the requirements of the hospital, overlooked the financial affairs and wrote the letters of the patients to their friends, oftentimes a word of comfort, a parting word for this world!

So this cannonading was a trial by fire for the Johanniters and the deaconesses in their field of labour, but they stood it bravely, as thousands of grateful tears and thousands of loving deeds which their example called forth testify.

The Hanoverian garrison in Altona helped the knights and the deaconesses as far as they could. One night, when the streets were as slippery as glass from ice, and the Johanniters were constantly carrying in fresh wounded on litters to their hospitals, the whole of the inhabitants voluntarily busied themselves in bringing sand in their hands, and handkerchiefs, and baskets, to scatter on the frozen paths.

Very soon Altona lay too far from the scene of the war, which moved rapidly northwards. The Johanniters erected in Flensburg a new hospital with fifty beds, and Anna with nine deaconesses proceeded thither. They came through Randsberg, and found there a war hospital under a Catholic doctor in a most comfortless condition. Anna and her deaconesses immediately offered their help; she never thought of the difference of creed, she only thought of her Christian duty to her poor wounded brethren. But the Catholic doctor was less large-hearted; he detained the sympathizing Protestant sisters for a long time with empty speeches until his Gray Sisters arrived, then he invited the deaconesses in mockery to a place in his field of work—in the kitchen and laundry and with the scullery-maids as servants to the Gray Sisters! So the Lady Mother of Bethany went on with her deaconesses to Flensburg, and answered not a word to the shameful mockery.

From the 15th of February, Anna and the nine sisters worked in the Johanniter hospital, Bellevue, which was situated high and beautifully over the town of Flensburg, and besides this managed three military hospitals erected there, one in the Latin School, one in a private house, and one in a hospital forsaken by the Danes; and containing sixty sorely wounded inmates. The first wounded in Bellevue were two Prussian and two Danish officers, but the daughter of the Stolbergs had no eye for the colour of the uniform, she only saw the fearful wounds beneath it, and these she dressed as lovingly for Danes as for Prussians.

With ever-increasing rapidity did the Prussians press towards the north, and more and more numerous were the sufferers to be tended. The various battles kept the hospitals full to overflowing, and gave the deaconesses work night and day. The Johanniters had one sailing vessel of their own for the transport of the wounded, and this, under the guidance of Knesebeck-Carve, conveyed constant relays of sufferers from the north to Flensburg.

In addition to the wounded there were a great many sick soldiers who had been prostrated by the severe winter weather, and the great prevalence of inflammation of the lungs and gastric fever. In the King's garden by the northern entrance to Flensburg, the Johanniters erected a new hospital with thirty beds, and Anna sent for more deaconesses from Bethany for it. At last she and twenty of her sisters were busy at the seat of war. To these were added in the beginning of March six nursing sisters, young ladies of noble families from Berlin, who in the great need had prepared themselves to be assistant eaconesses by the sick beds at Bethany.

It was very difficult for Anna to leave this work of love in the battle-field. She was indeed a daughter of the old Crusader, the brave blood of the Stolbergs flowed plentifully in the quiet deaconess; her eyes looked down from her high Bellevue to Duppel, the storming of which she would have liked to have seen with her own eyes, and to dress its wounded with her own hands. But, "Come, mother, come; your children cannot longer do without you!"—this was the ceaseless cry from Bethany; and so Anna, obedient to duty, returned to her children without having seen Prussia's banner waving on Duppel's citadel.

There was indeed much to be done and many to be nursed at Bethany. The quiet house had become a complete hospital. By the bedsides of numbers who had been able to bear the long journey, Anna continued the Samaritan work of the battle-field. And in addition to this she had to guide, to advise, to help, to strengthen the young sisters who had taken in Bethany the work of the absent deaconesses.

She writes from Berlin, where she had absorbing work in directing the hospital, to Altona, on February 12th: "Many thanks for your news about the dear hospitals, where my heart and thoughts often linger notwithstanding the overwhelming work inside and outside of this house. I heard yesterday that they were wondering in high places, why we offered no sisters to the Schleswig hospitals. I at once went off to the head physician, Dr. Grimm, about it, and he arranged for me to proceed to the Minister of War. He received me and was pleased at my offers, and said he would send for me when it was the right time, and would give us directions then. I offered— think of my bravery!—ten sisters. To-day I was at General Hering's to speak to him about the particulars; he thinks he would like to wait a little; but this evening I received a letter from the Minister of War directing us to proceed to Flensburg. I go thither joyfully in God's name, and am only sorry not to be able to set off to-morrow, but I must send for some distant sisters, so it will not be possible to go before Tuesday; this may be just as well, as I have a very bad cough and do not feel well. Whether Eberhard can accomplish his plan of placing us under the care of a knight, or whether he cannot, the whole matter appears to me rather dark, but I am not afraid, for the Lord will never forsake his little flock."

From Bethany she writes, on April 18th, to Flensburg: "I have now been ten years a deaconess, would that I could be one in every respect! I follow our dear Eberhard in spirit, the Lord will shelter and shield him from all evil. I have appropriated the 91st Psalm to him, and have been strengthened and comforted by its precious promises. What may be happening when this letter reaches your hand! The Governor of Jena is already dead, our two dear dying ones here are still sinking. I think much of the precious invalids. May the Lord, the Prince of Life, be gracious to them, and cure them for all eternity!"

And then on April 22nd: "My heart dances and jumps for joy and thankfulness, and triumph and deep emotion, while I thank our merciful Lord for the wonders of his power and majesty. I do it here in my loneliness, from the depths of my soul, yet you will believe me that I feel more as if with you than here. Louise and Agnes have already gone. Are there enough sisters yet? I can send two more lay sisters—oh that I could send myself! But that cannot be; I must not even think of it, or I get too sorry about it. N—— told us so much that was beautiful and wonderfully touching. How many many sick we have at Bellevue and Dally! How melancholy it must be for all who have no hope! Oh that the Lord may guide them to his eternal kingdom, and cause many to be cured in our two dear houses! To-day the King will have visited them all; how I envy him and you and the sisters! May the Lord enable the latter to do their duty in these times of great distress and suffering, and give me grace here for my duties."

Count Eberhard Stolberg worked ceaselessly with his knights at the seat of war for more than half a year. His younger brother, Count Bolko, was busy in the hospital at Kolding, and, like a true knight's lady, the Countess Eberhard stood all the time by her husband's side to help him.

Scarcely were the last wounded in the Danish war healed, before the cannons in Bohemia summoned the Johanniters and the deaconesses to fresh activity. Anna conducted her sisters to the new hospital at Gorlitz. When she had arranged and settled all there with indefatigable industry, she returned to the war hospital at Bethany, where the nursing sisters from the Danish war resumed their work of love, while the Bethany deaconesses found in Bohemia a great field of labour.

The King of Prussia wished to reward the superintendent and sisters of Bethany who had wrought such marvels of courage and brotherly love on the fields of honour with the war medal, but Anna's humility gratefully declined this worldly decoration. "Not unto us, Lord, not unto us, but unto thy name be the glory," was the rule of her whole life.

What the Johanniters under their leader, who was placed by the King's command at the head of all the relief societies, accomplished, has become a matter of history.

Eberhard and Anna Stolberg, shadowing and fruit-bearing branches, cover a wide country. Yes, the prophetical prayer of the pious shopwoman behind the tower of St. Gall was wonderfully fulfilled!

CHAPTER XII.

RHEIN.

"Greater love hath no man than this, that a man lay down his life for his friends."—JOHN xv. 13.

"WE are hungry! we are hungry! Your poor brethren in East Prussia are starving!" Since the spring of 1867 this wail of sorrow had sounded through the land, almost unheeded by the wealthy.

"We are hungry! we are perishing! we are falling victims to famine fever! We are hungry! we are perishing!" The wail sounded louder and louder as the winter began; it was a praying, imploring, pleading, threatening cry!

In April, 1867, famine fever, or, more

M

properly, typhus fever, which had been partly produced by want of food, though it might have had other causes too, broke out among the labourers on the Southern Railway between Bartenstein and Rastenberg; for they were herded together in the most wretched, bare, mud hovels, surrounded by filth, and injuring their health with unwholesome and unnourishing food.

Another harvest-time passed away, ruined by the pouring rain. With the growing hunger, fever grew rapidly too. The starving people, in begging, spread the infection, by their persons and clothing, throughout the famishing country; farther and farther did the powerful poison spread, a poison even more catching than that of cholera. But the misery had not reached its highest point; to the hunger, to the typhus, was added a third grim spectre—stern cold winter and no wood for firing, no proper shelter, no wholesome or sufficient nourishment, no warm bed, no clean linen, no medicine, no stimulants for the sick, no protecting clothing for the well!

These three spectres appeared in the most awful way in some of the provinces shortly before Christmas, among a terribly poor population, who were quite among the lowest of the Prussian kingdom in culture or civilisation, and who spent their dull, heavy lives vegetating in ignorance and infidelity and in an almost animal state of dirt.

No energetic effort was made against these three spectres who attacked the poor people with ever-increasing deadliness, and branded them with their fatal mark; no sanitary commission attempted to root out the hungertyphus from the plague-infested dwellings by compulsory cleaning and kind nursing and help; no police rules hindered the spread of the poison by the wandering beggars; no sufficient hospital existed. The proud town of Rastenberg, with its five thousand inhabitants, lying on the direct railway route, called a miserable dirty hut in the midst of manure heaps its county hospital. The hospital of Tapiau consisted of two small dirty rooms, in one of which lay seven hopeless cases of typhus in the most miserable beds or on filthy straw, and in the other close beside them, only separated by a door which would not shut, lay five sick women, none of whom had typhus as yet. Their nurses were a sick man—who himself stood sorely in need of help, who could scarcely step from one bed to another—and an old weak woman.

But not in vain did the cry of distress from the hungry, starving brethren resound in the distance. From all sides kind hearts and open hands offered themselves, and the Johanniters were again among the first to help. They sent doctors, wine, an iron stove, and woollen clothing; they arranged for the right distribution of the sums entrusted to them; they enlarged their hospitals in Prussia, Holland, and Bartenstein, fed day by day the hungry children in the schools, distributed everywhere food and medicine, and, what was more, gave themselves to the work. They left their comfortable home life and went to help their poor suffering brethren on their filthy sick beds in the poisonous pest-holes reeking with the atmosphere of death.

But what can men do, even when accustomed to the nursing of the wounded in the battle-field, when called to the bedsides of women and children raving in the wild delirium of typhus? The softer hands of women were needed there.

"Anna, help us! help us and these poor creatures!" was the cry that reached Bethany again from the Count Eberhard; and the call did not fall in vain on his sister's ear. Although Bethany, besides its normal number of two hundred and sixty cases, had had to nurse about three hundred patients in consequence of the winter's wide-spread sickness and misery, and the sisters had had to work to the utmost of their strength, yet Anna was able to help once more. On the evening of January 17th, she and two sisters set out for Rhein. Two others followed to assist the almost worn-out deaconesses in the hospitals of Gerdauen and Bartenstein. Late at night on January 20th they reached their destination, and found an amount of misery no pen can describe.

Rhein is a peculiarly poor little village. To its usual distressed inhabitants were added hundreds of poor railway labourers, who, at the commencement of the severe winter, crouched together in their dirty mud huts round the village, without work or bread, hungry and famishing, and trying to keep themselves warm by thus huddling together in the frightful cold. Typhus soon raged fearfully in these pestilential dens, without fireplaces or any ventilation. Sick and well, dying and dead, lay close together, and no one from the town itself troubled themselves about these unhappy ones.

They needed bread, clothing, warmth, medicine, doctors—everything! The two doctors who, on the outbreak of the fever, had self-denyingly devoted themselves to their duties, lay ill from the fever. There was no idea of any organized system of nursing. In this sore time of trouble the knight Von Tyszka, obedient to the principles of the Johanniters, arrived at Rhein; he established himself in the unfortunate village, and took the nursing in hand. But how was he to begin in this terrible plight, seeing he could not expect the smallest help from the local authorities? The noble man did not hesitate long, he began where there was the greatest distress. A brave citizen of Rhein, a merchant, Hofer by name, joined him, and both men penetrated, at the risk of their lives, into the wretched mud hovels full of pestilential air, and carried the sickest of the sick, the most miserable of the miserable, out of them in their arms, into warm dry rooms, where they provided them with food and medicine. But what more could these two well do? And yet there was immeasurably more to be done in the wretched dwellings of the poor in the town.

Then, like a delivering angel, the Mother of Bethany and her two deaconesses arrived. They found forty typhus cases in the temporary hospital of the Johanniters all crowded into two rooms, one for men the other for women and children. Two and three patients lay in each bed, most of them only on straw, hardly covered with rags, stiff with dirt and infested with vermin; while round dying mothers crouched alike their sick and their well children.

Still more deplorable, however, was the state of the labourers' dwellings in the town, where frequently six families, numbering twenty or thirty men and women, girls and boys, sick and well, all half naked, were huddled together in a small noisome room on dirty straw scattered on the unboarded, damp mud floor. Perished with cold, devoured by vermin, and almost starved, haunted by the phantasies of typhus or moaning with the pain of frost-bites, cursing God and the world and themselves, or lying in obstinate silence, every one of them expected but one deliverer—Death! "My heart stood still when first I entered these pest-holes; I never saw such human misery!" remarked Anna afterwards.

But her heart had no time to stand still; useless exclamations and condolence would not benefit these miserable beings, it was necessary to run quickly and energetically to help them; and to work earnestly day and night for them, and this Anna and her sisters did with a self-denial and devotion beyond all compare, and almost passing the strength of men. "They accomplish an incredible amount," wrote an eye-witness from Rhein.

Still the unsympathizing municipality did not bestir itself at all. So Anna and the Johanniters provided roomy, light, airy hospital wards, and bought, begged, and borrowed bedsteads, and bedclothes, and woollen coverings, and other necessary furniture. They sat up till late in the night, making mattresses and shirts, until at last they really did get help in this part of their work from some ladies in the town, whose lethargic hearts were shamed and shaken out of their indifference, by the noble example of the foreign deaconesses.

Directly a clean bed was ready in the hospital, Anna and the sisters bathed a patient, cleaned him from the terrible vermin, and dressed him comfortably for it. The greatest caution was requisite in moving the sick to the new house on account of the exceedingly severe weather, but they very soon had sixty typhus cases under their care. First came the women and children, then the men. Then the work of nursing began, and Martha and Mary went quietly from one sick brother to another, untroubled by the fact that every breath from those beds contained deadly poison for themselves. The action of this typhus poison is so much the more fearful that its virulence increases by the daily contact with the sick, till it breaks out in its full, awful power.

Anna was not, however, satisfied even with

this work. She went again and again to the breeding-places of the disease, to the dirt-empoisoned dwellings of the poor inhabitants, and tried, notwithstanding the almost incredible opposition of the people, who had grown up in filth and ignorance, to separate at once the sick from the well, to clean their rooms, to admit fresh air, and to provide proper clothing for those likely to fall a prey to the fever. Both the men and the women particularly objected to the opening of the windows and doors, which were usually most carefully kept shut the entire winter. Only when the patients were dying did their relatives permit their removal to what, with almost childish amazement, they called "the hospital of the white ladies." Frequently this removal had to be forcibly effected, and then the convalescents had to be removed out of the hospital almost as forcibly, so happy had they been under the motherly, loving nursing of the foreign ladies.

Not even at night was there rest for Anna and her deaconesses. If they tried to strengthen themselves by some hours' sleep in their poor little room at the inn, they heard groans all night in the next room, for there lay one of the two sick doctors in the wild delirium of fever.

Anna had only four days to arrange the hospital at Rhein. Though herself somewhat unwell the last day, she worked unceasingly. Then she had to write the letters home from this abode of misery, and these were always fresh and brave, and full of God's comfort. She left Rhein on January 25th, followed by the blessings of the poor patients. She knew they would be well cared for by the faithful hands of her two deaconesses and the indefatigable Johanniter, Tuszka. Her feelings of increasing illness prevented her from visiting the Johanniter hospital in Holland, as she had at first intended. Perhaps an unknown presentiment drew her back to her dear Bethany, that she might not die among strangers. At all events she returned home most unexpectedly on the 28th of January.

The joy of the reunion, the happiness of being once more at home, made her at first forget the threatened symptoms of illness. She told all about her adventures with great freshness, and at the wish of Queen Elizabeth visited Charlottenburg, to give this true friend a minute description of the distress in East Prussia. She rejoiced like a child at the hundred thalers which her brother Eberhard sent for her nurslings at Rhein, and went in happy activity from shop to shop, making purchases of linen and clothing, and dispatching them to Rhein. She seemed to have no time to be ill. Already Count

Eberhard had called again: "Anna, help us; your deaconesses are not enough for Rhein!"

With her usually firm, clear, beautiful handwriting (a picture of her life), she wrote back to her brother on February 1st: "Dear Eberhard, we are sending three more sisters to Rhein. If Kaiserswerth and Breslau refuse, we shall consider it our duty to do our utmost; but at present it does not appear possible to send out more deaconesses from Bethany. Still, when there is no help, God gives his help, and all becomes possible."

.And so it proved. When the two first sisters both lay very ill at Rhein, smitten down by typhus, Anna, from her own sick bed, sent other sisters to Rhein, who found the self-denying Johanniter struck down too.

On the 4th of February, the same day on which, fourteen years before, she had entered on her duties, she partook of the Lord's Supper in the chapel at Bethany with her very aged mother, who loved to come over from her widowed home at Potsdam on such occasions, and seemed greatly to enjoy the sermon on Simeon's words, "Lord, now lettest thou thy servant depart in peace."

It was a sadly prophetical word for the anniversary of her thirteen-year-old happy and toilsome work, a fitting termination to a life rich in blessing.

It was only by the exertion of all her strength that she managed to be present next day at a meeting about the sending of another sister to Rhein and the reception of two probationers, and then at an interview with the secretary of the Johanniters in Prussia, Count Schlobitten, about the undertaking a hospital in East Prussia. She gave her whole mind to this last act of her duties; then the sick, fevered body demanded its rights. She sank on her sick bed, never to rise again from it. Hers was a truly blessed and instructive illness, for she had indeed laid down her life for her brethren.

CHAPTER XIII.

BETHANY.

"Little children, it is the last time."—1 JOHN ii. 18.

NOBODY in Bethany dreamed that their beloved mother was already summoned from them, and from the service here to the eternal reward above. She alone realised it from the first hour of her illness. It was such a blessed prospect to her; out of work and conflict into rest and peace, out of weakness into glory. From one morning watch to another she had longingly waited for her Lord, now her soul bounded forth to meet Him.

During her increasing illness, she often

said to the sisters, "Do not pray me back from the Lord."

"But, mother, would you not wish to remain a little longer with us? We need you so much."

"If it be the Lord's will—just what He wills." Her complete self-resignation was strong to the very end.

On Thursday evening she asked the nurse to send for the lawyer of the house, "but quite quietly, so as not to alarm the dear sisters." She wished to set her house in order. The nurse tried to persuade her to postpone it till the next morning, but she replied, "Let me do it, I do not know whether I shall be able to-morrow." To the hastily summoned lawyer she handed very peacefully the will she had written and sealed with her own hand some years before, in which she devoted half of her fortune to the endowment of the Marianne Institution in her Silesian home, and the other half to her last earthly home, Bethany. When the lawyer prudently asked her whether the will was quite in correct form, she smiled. "Oh, yes, I had the advice of a very competent authority at my side." On the opening of her will afterwards, however, owing to a slight flaw, it would have been found invalid, had not her family sanctioned its full performance.

The perfect peace of mind with which she awaited the casting aside of her mortal part continued with her to the end. She sometimes said, with a smile, "I should like to know who our dear God has chosen as my successor." In order, however, not to influence the choice of the authorities, she never mentioned the name which in her heart she wished to belong to the head of Bethany, but her eyes lit up, even in her last moments, when they rested on the sweet, sorrowful face of the Sister Amelia. Her unspoken wish was gratified. The whole community unanimously selected Sister Amelia Platen, who for many years had worked devotedly as Anna's assistant, to be their " mother."

It was touching to see how Anna conquered her own great pain, so as not to grieve others by it. Although, on account of the ceaseless cough and the inflammation on her lungs, with which spotted typhus often begins, as well as the great fever and headache and weariness, it only hurt her to take food from time to time, yet she always complied with the entreaties of the nursing sister to do so. She often spoke lovingly and solicitously about the poor patients at Bethany, especially the little children. Her headache was so violent that she generally lay with closed eyes; but she never complained, she only apologized to Sister Catherine, because "her head was so extremely bad." She remembered her sister Charlotte's birthday, and sent her her blessing and a bouquet, and spoke with great sympathy of the Sister Rosalie, who had had to follow her father to the grave on her very birthday. She prepared herself with all her power for her mother's visit, so as not to appear too ill, "that my darling mother may not be too troubled." She asked the nursing sister to tell her sister-in-law, the Countess Eberhard, of her illness, "but treat it lightly."

From her sick bed she cared like a true mother for all her household, and gave the minutest directions about the erection of a dwelling for the physician. She sent a message to the renowned surgeon of Bethany, Wilms, who was going to Wiesbaden for his health, asking him to come and say farewell to her. She was thinking of a different farewell to what was in the mind of the departing doctor. Her self-denial made her wish at first to lighten the nursing and night watching of the sisters, and she used to say, " Children, you must not stay with me ;" but afterwards she gently and affectionately accepted their service of love. " If they will do it, I am very satisfied," she remarked, for she saw that it grieved the sisters to be away from her.

She was so pleased to see again some sisters who had just returned from a distance, and humbly asked forgiveness from one whom she had misjudged some time before. "You do not believe," she remarked, "how our sins stand like mountains before us at such an hour." "But, mother, the good God just wants poor sinners who have been washed clean in Christ's blood." "That is my only comfort," she replied, with a radiant face.

She delighted in preparing with her pastor for her " going home." She used to drink in God's Word, and liked to have the Bible and the hymn-book of the house read to her.

In her sleep she repeated the words of one old hymn of comfort. She always lay with folded hands as if in prayer. Her face had such a wonderful radiancy of peace, that the bystanders could hardly look at her. Even in her delirium she prayed and repeated hymns. With the last strength she had, she cast from her the smallest praise for her works on earth. "No, no, it was all of grace," she cried, with all her heart, and then quoted the words, "Here lies a poor sinner who has been made happy by a great ransom."

She looked back on her own life very thankfully. "I am not worthy of the faithfulness and love the Lord hath shown me. The lot fell to me in pleasant places; I have had a lovely home on earth."

She was very grateful during her illness for the smallest service done for her by a sister, and even when her lips could no longer express her thanks, her eyes beamed as she pressed their hands.

She showed the first spots of typhus on February 8th. It was beyond a doubt that she had imbibed the fatal poison by the sick beds at Rhein. It almost seemed as if she was glad at this certainty that her longings would be satisfied. She often counted the days to the 11th of February, which was the day on which her father had died, and she hoped to go home the same day; but this was not to be. Her illness increased with fearful rapidity; she became delirious. She fancied herself at Rhein or on the journey home, and used to crave for her dear Bethany. "God be praised, I can see my Bethany now. I am inside the grounds now. Oh, I shall not die away from it;" and her eyes sparkled still more brightly. In the greatness of her fever she used to cry for a cool shady, resting-place. Once she said, when very restless, "Oh, I wish I could lie quite still!" She often spoke with pleasure of her happy work on earth. Her eyes used to search in her delirium for Bethany, and then, when she recognised her sleeping-room and the loved faces of the sisters, a look of perfect peace used to come over her features. She repeatedly called for her mother and brothers and sisters. One night she said, "The Lord is taking my work away from me; I know it, but I know too it is the right hour when He calls." After a bad night she said, "Every night is like a piece of a dark valley; but the Lord is with me!"

She greeted the first bleeding at the nose (a symptom she had known so well at the death-beds at Rhein) with great delight: "Just one more step to my freedom."

With ever-increasing rapidity did this freedom come. The fever consumed her small remaining strength. On Sunday evening, February 16th, she was lying calmly and peacefully. The struggle was over. All the sisters in the house stood with her two brothers, Counts Eberhard and Theodore, praying quietly round her bed. Just at midnight the ransomed soul went gently home, amidst the sobs of the watchers.

Sisters watched by the dear remains. The room was not empty the whole day, so many wished to gaze once more on the still face radiant with heavenly brightness. And sisters carried the corpse to the last service in the chancel of the church. By it were spoken these words: "What more beautiful ending could our mother have had? A friend has called it a heroine's death. She obeyed the Apostle's words, 'We ought to lay down our lives for the brethren;' but she never thought about it. Washed clean in the blood of the Lamb, given to the Lord, that was all. She died as simply as a child."

Soon after her death the Bethany deaconesses found a very precious parting letter from their mother. It was as follows:—

"To my dear Sisters.

"When you read these lines my heart will no longer be beating, for the Lord will have called his humble handmaiden away from her happy service and away from the duties among which He had placed her. He has been very gracious to me in pardoning my many and great sins for Christ's sake, and in drawing me to himself, and so enabling me to believe and hope in Him.

"My dear sisters, I bid you farewell in the Lord's name, and I pray and beseech you, my children, to abide in Him, and to be full of love to each other. That is my last wish, my last bequest to you.

"May God bestow on you all the spirit of love and truth. I thank you with all my heart for every kindness and all the love which I have always received as an undeserved gift of mercy from God, and for which I have thanked Him in private. I ask your forgiveness for everything in which I have vexed you or given you offence, and for all the sins of omission and commission in which I have erred against you; forgive me for Christ our Lord's sake, as I hope and believe He has forgiven me. I commend you to his grace, and trust myself simply and solely to the blood wherewith He has redeemed me. Do not weep for my death, the Lord will not leave you orphans, but has already chosen for you another, who will be a true mother and a great blessing to you. Help her in her heavy but precious work, as you have helped me by your loving obedience.

"I implore God's rich grace and blessing on my dear successor. May our dear, dear Bethany be built up by her, and may it become increasingly known, far and wide, as a house of peace and mercy, chosen and blessed by the Lord himself. And so may our faithful, gracious God keep and bless you, and cause us all to meet again in his presence with exceeding joy. The grace of the Lord Jesus be with you all.

" ANNA.

"Bethany, February, 1856."

CHAPTER XIV.

CONCLUSION.

THE same want of ostentation which had marked her whole life was observed in the carrying of Anna from the house to the grave. "Very quietly and without any show, just like one of the deaconesses"—this had been her direction in her last will.

But the simple ceremony could not be quite so quiet and unnoticed as she in her humility had desired. Love and gratitude would not suffer themselves to be driven back—the love and gratitude which had bound the highest and the lowest to the deceased in the same strong way. King

William, with his own hand, laid a shining laurel crown next the maiden myrtle wreath which lay on the black cloth covered coffin of her who had been the self-sacrificing nurse of his wounded soldiers in war, and of his sick subjects in peace. The Queens Augusta and Elizabeth added to the laurel of bravery and renown the white roses and camellias of love; and when the hundreds of high-born mourners had passed away from the peaceful churchyard, there entered very timidly many, many of the poor, to cast secretly on the quiet form a modest wreath of snowdrops, a little spray of rosemary, or the one little rosebud from the flowerpot in the window at home, and almost tremblingly they laid these simple gifts on the bright laurel and the mass of costly wreaths and flowers, while tears of love and gratitude flowed from their eyes at the thought of the mother of the poor and sick who lay at rest there.

Yes, the unostentatious funeral testified more than words what the mother of Bethany had been to the wide world, notwithstanding her quiet, unassuming ways, and her own great dislike to publicity.

The church at Bethany could hardly hold all the mourners of all classes. The King and Queen and the whole household were present. The widowed Queen Elizabeth, suffering as she did from painful lameness, was carried there on her couch to prove her love to the daughters of Anton Stolberg and to the mother of her dear poor.

In the midst of her sons and daughters, and all the remaining Stolbergs, the grey-haired mother in her eighty-first year wept tears of hope for the daughter who had gone before her.

All the Johanniters who were in Berlin assembled to do the last honours to the truest of " Hospitallers." The heads of the Prussian

Church, of the Prussian State, of the Prussian army, showed by their presence how inexpressibly great had been their loss by the departure of this modest worker from among them. The members of the nobility honoured and mourned in the deceased at once as the noble daughter of the Stolbergs, the sister of their esteemed Count Eberhard zu Stolberg, the truest patriot and the most faithful handmaiden of the Lord, the heroine who had laid down her life for her brethren. The inmates of the deaconess establishment, with their pale, sorrowful faces, filled the whole nave of the church; and the swollen eyes of the numbers of poor, present, bore testimony to their love for their precious departed mother.

All eyes rested on the simple coffin before the altar, with the seven-branched golden candelabra beside it, standing in the same place where, thirteen years before, the Deaconess Anna was dedicated to her office as head of Bethany. And by this coffin the chaplain of Bethany, who had buried Count Anton Stolberg, drew a telling picture of the life of the departed one; and by this coffin they sang the same hymns they had sung by the coffin of her father, "Jesus is my confidence," "Oh, let Thy grace abide with me," &c.

She had herself chosen the text for her funeral sermon (John xvi. 33); but her wish was mentioned to the chaplain too late for him to comply with it. After the prayer and blessing, the King accompanied the grey-haired mother after the coffin, which was placed in a hearse drawn by only two white horses. Next to them came the Stolbergs, then the weeping deaconesses with wreaths and crosses of flowers, and then a mourning procession of more than a hundred carriages at the head of which was the royal mourning coach. In the last carriage sat General von Ollech, who had been cured of his battle wounds by the excellent nursing at Bethany.

In all the streets through which the cortège passed, there stood on both sides a respectful, quiet crowd of people, and many eyes were wet, and many a head bowed reverentially as they passed on through the wintry streets of Berlin to the Louisenstadtischen churchyard. Here Anna had long ago chosen a quiet, green resting place in the midst of the fourteen sisters who had died before her; in the free earth, under the open sky, a true daughter of the old Counts sleeping in the churchyard of St. Theobald's little church at Wernigerode.

By the open grave the sisters sang or sobbed the favourite hymns of their mother, "Lord Jesus, Thy dear blood," and after a prayer, "Rejoice, O my soul." A shower of flowers covered the coffin when it was let down, and then the grave was quickly closed.

It is a wonderfully peaceful, quiet little spot in the churchyard where the Bethany deaconesses rest from their labours. A simple iron railing, blooming with creeping plants, encloses a long piece of turf. Two benches invite to a prolonged resting time by the graves.' Already fifteen green hillocks over deaconesses who have gone home are ranged side by side. A little white tablet at the head tells the time of death, and the text which was the favourite of the departed one when on earth; nothing more—no eulogies, no worldly praise.

In the midst of these graves a tall, white marble cross stands conspicuous. Beneath it lie two graves, one old and richly covered with grass, with the little tablet:—

MARIANNE VON RANTZEN,
5TH JANUARY, 1855.
Romans xiv. 8.

And next it a fresh hillock, which is covered by four springs' fresh green covering, and is always adorned with the wreaths loving hands place there. A weeping willow bends its branches over it; its inscription is—

ANNA, COUNTESS ZU STOLBERG WERNIGERODE,
17TH FEBRUARY, 1868.
1 John i. 7.

All the flowers on the hillock will fade and can be blighted by a breath of wind; the white marble with the name Anna zu Stolberg Wernigerode will get weather-beaten, and the grave will vanish from the face of the earth; the pages of this little book, which are such feeble descriptions of the marvellous scenes of a life so full of love, and so calculated to be a joy to believers, a comfort to mourners, a strength to the humble, a warning to the unfaithful, a call to the sleeping, and a mirror to the self-pleasing, will pass away; but the abiding influences of her actions and the memory of her life of whole-hearted devotedness can never be effaced from the annals of time or eternity.

THE END.

LONDON: PRINTED BY VIRTUE AND CO., CITY ROAD.

LIST OF BOOKS

PUBLISHED BY

STRAHAN AND CO.,

56, LUDGATE HILL, LONDON.

By the DUKE of ARGYLL.

1. THE REIGN OF LAW. Crown 8vo, 6s. People's Edition. Limp cloth, 2s. 6d.
2. PRIMEVAL MAN. An Examination of some Recent Speculations. Crown 8vo, 4s. 6d.
3. IONA. With Illustrations. Crown 8vo, 3s. 6d.

By the late THOMAS GUTHRIE, D.D.

1. STUDIES OF CHARACTER FROM THE OLD TESTAMENT. First and Second Series, crown 8vo, 3s. 6d. each.
2. THE PARABLES READ IN THE LIGHT OF THE PRESENT DAY. Crown 8vo, 3s. 6d.
3. MAN AND THE GOSPEL. Crown 8vo, 3s. 6d.
4. OUR FATHER'S BUSINESS. Crown 8vo, 3s. 6d.
5. OUT OF HARNESS. Crown 8vo, 3s. 6d.
6. SPEAKING TO THE HEART. Crown 8vo, 3s. 6d.
7. THE ANGELS' SONG. 18mo, 1s. 6d.
8. EARLY PIETY. 18mo, 1s. 6d.
9. SUNDAYS ABROAD. Crown 8vo, 3s. 6d.
10. SAVING KNOWLEDGE. Addressed to Young Men. By the late THOMAS GUTHRIE, D.D., and W. G. BLAIKIE, D.D. Crown 8vo, 3s. 6d.

By GEORGE MAC DONALD, LL.D.

1. ANNALS OF A QUIET NEIGHBOURHOOD. Crown 8vo, 6s.
2. THE SEABOARD PARISH. Crown 8vo, 6s.
3. WILFRID CUMBERMEDE. Crown 8vo, 6s.
4. THE DISCIPLE, and other Poems. Crown 8vo, 6s.
5. UNSPOKEN SERMONS. Crown 8vo, 3s. 6d.
6. THE MIRACLES OF OUR LORD. Crown 8vo, 5s.
7. RANALD BANNERMAN'S BOYHOOD. With Illustrations. Crown 8vo, cloth extra, 5s.
8. AT THE BACK OF THE NORTH WIND. With Illustrations. Crown 8vo, cloth gilt extra, 5s.
9. WORKS OF FANCY AND IMAGINATION; being a Reprint of Poetical and other Works. Pocket Volume Edition, in neat case, £2 2s.

By the late NORMAN MACLEOD, D.D.

1. PEEPS AT THE FAR EAST. An Account of a Visit to India. With Illustrations. Square 8vo, cloth gilt extra, 21s.
2. EASTWARD. Travels in Egypt, Syria, and Palestine. With Illustrations. Crown 8vo, 6s.
3. THE STARLING. With Illustrations. Crown 8vo, 6s.
4. REMINISCENCES OF A HIGHLAND PARISH. Crown 8vo, 6s.
5. THE OLD LIEUTENANT AND HIS SON. With Illustrations. Crown 8vo, 3s. 6d.
6. THE EARNEST STUDENT. Memorials of John Mackintosh. Crown 8vo, 3s. 6d.
7. THE GOLD THREAD. With Illustrations. Square 8vo, 2s. 6d.
8. THE TEMPTATION OF OUR LORD. Crown 8vo, 5s.

By C. J. VAUGHAN, D.D.,
MASTER OF THE TEMPLE.

1. FAMILY PRAYERS. Crown 8vo, 3s. 6d.
2. SUNDAYS IN THE TEMPLE. Small 8vo, 3s. 6d.
3. HALF-HOURS IN THE TEMPLE CHURCH. Small 8vo, 3s. 6d.
4. LAST WORDS IN THE PARISH CHURCH OF DONCASTER. Crown 8vo, 3s. 6d.
5. EARNEST WORDS FOR EARNEST MEN. Small 8vo, 3s. 6d.
6. THE PRESENCE OF GOD IN HIS TEMPLE. Small 8vo, 3s. 6d.

L. STRAHAN AND CO., 56, LUDGATE HILL, LONDON.

www.ingramcontent.com/pod-product-compliance
Lightning Source LLC
Chambersburg PA
CBHW020907230426
43666CB00008B/1351